COFFEE SOMMELIER

A VOYAGE THROUGH CULTURE AND RITES OF COFFEE

WHITE STAR PUBLISHERS

COFFEE MUST BE HOT AS HELL,

BLACK AS THE DEVIL,

PURE AS AN ANGEL AND SWEET AS LOVE.

- Mikhail Alexandrovich Bakunin -

TEXT BY LUIGI ODELLO

PHOTOGRAPHS BY FABIO PETRONI

RECIPES BY CHEF GIOVANNI RUGGIERI

Project editor VALERIA MANFERTO DE FABIANIS

Editorial assistant LAURA ACCOMAZZO

Graphic design MARIA CUCCHI

CONTENTS

6-7 Detail of a 1855 Viennese coffee machine.

14-15 An old coffee grinder.

PAIRING COFFEE AND FOOD   PAGE   192

20 RECIPES BY CHEF GIOVANNI RUGGIERI

ALPHABETICAL INDEX
OF RECIPE INGREDIENTS

THE AUTHORS

COFFEE

Simply extraordinary. What, you ask? The answer is coffee, of course. And the reasons why it is so extraordinary are not hard to explain.

Among one of the world's most popular drinks, coffee made its first appearance around the fourteenth century in Yemen, where it was cultivated. But more or less a century before that, we know that in Ethiopia, coffee's country of origin, this plant used to grow spontaneously. Why coffee took so long to become a consumer good we do not know, but what we do know is that today coffee is the world's second product on the international market, after oil. We drink about 700 billion cups of coffee a year, which are made out of the over 137 million hundredweights (7 billion kilos) of green coffee coming from the over 30 million cultivations in 75 countries across the tropical bean belt. These figures are huge, especially considering they are the result of less than two centuries of coffee history: in 1825, the volume of coffee production was about ninety times inferior and today it just keeps on growing.

The origin of this world phenomenon is the Coffea, a shrub that botanists include in the Rubiaceae family and that branches into over ninety species of which only two account for most of the world's total production: Coffea Arabica and Coffea Canephora (commonly known as Robusta coffee) that due to natural mutation and partly to man's care and skill, have become the progenitors of over seventy coffee varieties. And if we multiply these varieties by the variables depending on the territory (such as climate, exposition and soil) we end up with a number of coffee qualities that almost equals those of vines. But that is not all, because then there are different cultivation methods, harvesting practices, and coffee bean processing techniques: namely spontaneous coffee plants growing in forests in shady patches under large trees and vast orderly plantations, selectively hand-picked or stripped drupes harvested from the branches, and powerful machines passing over the plantation automatically harvesting rows of coffee plants: every method will deliver different sensorial properties in our cup of coffee.

Another extraordinary aspect of coffee is the fact that usually the pulp of the coffee cherry goes to waste and all that is used are the seeds, what we know as the coffee beans. The drupe – that is the scientific name for the cherry around the beans – is in fact composed of an outer skin, a sweet pulp and typically two (but sometimes only one) seeds, the coffee beans, positioned with their two flat sides adjoined. To produce coffee as we know it, the beans must be removed from the pulp, and there are three different methods to carry out this process, each delivering a different kind of result in terms of product, namely un-washed, semi-washed, and washed coffee.

Once the parchment and the silver skin around the beans are removed, the beans are ready to be roasted. And this is where other important factors come into play, variables that will determine the taste and the aroma of the coffee we will sip from our cup: different processes, different timings, and different temperatures will deliver different sensorial properties and different flavors. After roasting comes the grinding of the roasted beans, which is another important step, although not quite as crucial as the brewing: there are at least ten completely different ways of preparing a cup of coffee, each one with its own characteristics.

In short: no matter how much effort you might put into it, one lifetime will never be enough to taste all the different varieties coffee has to offer. And we didn't even consider all the possible combinations coffee lends itself to, namely with milk, spirits, you name it.

And that is why coffee is so extraordinary.

WHERE IS COFFEE CULTIVATED AND HOW

THE PLANT, THE PLANTS

The genus Coffea includes an extraordinary range of species, but only two of them are interesting as far as fruits suitable for human consumption: the Arabica and the Canephora species, the latter commonly known as Robusta. Two species that thrive in very different climate conditions and habit and that, above all, once brewed, deliver very different beverages.

ROBUSTA

Compared to Arabica, Canephora is less widespread, perhaps less refined, but certainly more resistant, to parasites especially. And perhaps this is the reason why in 1900 it was named Robusta precisely to describe its robustness, a quality that can also be tasted in the coffee that is made with it, which is in fact generally more bitter, astringent and full-bodied than Arabica as it contains greater quantities of caffeine (2–3.5%) and phenolic acids. The height of a spontaneous Canephora plant can range between 23 and 42 feet (7–13 meters). In cultivations the height is obviously inferior. Its leaves are fine and elliptical and it grows particularly visible round cherries. Robusta is cultivated between an altitude of 650 and 1900 feet (200–600 meters) since this plant does not love the temperature excursions typical of higher elevations and prefers constant temperatures between 75 °F and 85 °F (24–29 °C). This plant, that was among the first species to appear on our planet, has 24 chromosomes and is allogamous, meaning that its flowers require an external intervention to carry out pollination.

ARABICA

Arabica is certainly the most widespread species, although the spread of Robusta is on the rise, due to its adaptability to inhospitable climates (today more frequent due to climate change) and to the increasing demand of lesser quality coffee. The height of an Arabica plant can range between 9 and 16 feet (3–5 meters), but in plantations its height is limited between 6 to 9 feet (2–3 meters) for harvesting purposes. Its trunk is smooth and straight with long fine branches and lanceolate coriaceous leaves. Inside the lower part of the ovary, which is split in two, are two ovules from which the coffee beans originate.

The Arabica species easily adapts to different environmental conditions, does not tolerate frost, likes the change of season, and can grow at an altitude between 2900 and 6500 feet (900–2000 meters), where temperatures range between 60 °F and 75 °F (15–24 °C). Compared to Robusta, Arabica grows beans with less caffeine (0.7–2%), higher percentage of sugar and fats combined with important aroma precursors: a set of characteristics that make Arabica a favorite among most coffee enthusiasts.

The origin of this species was accidental when the number of chromosomes of an existing species grew to 48 making the plant autogamous, that is to say capable of self-pollination (although cross-pollination does occur in Arabica plants with incidence rates between 10–20%).

The Coffee Tree.

If in the world of winemaking it is arduous to make a general discourse about vines – since they are in fact varieties and there are hundreds of them – the same is true when it comes to coffee because over the centuries, either due nature or to human intervention, Arabica and Robusta have originated different sub-species or new species resulting from their cross-breeding.

In the ambit of the genus Coffea, however, things are more complicated com-pared to those of the genus Vitis, since in the coffee sector there has been less codification and often (more often than for wines, anyway) varietals have been named after a region and so it is hard to tell if a denomination simply refers to a territory or to a genetically different population.

Here follows a description of some of the main varieties selected among the over fifty varietals of the Arabica family and the twenty of the Canephora family that are relevant in the coffee production industry.

BOURBON. Alongside Typica, Bourbon is the one of the cultivars from which many other Arabica varieties are bred. Created in the eighteenth century on the island of Réunion, that was formerly known as Île Bourbon in the Indian Ocean east of Madagascar, Bourbon cultivations arrived in Brazil in the late nineteenth century, rapidly spreading across the continent. Bourbon has a low yield poten-tial and grows coffee beans that are highly appreciated. Red, Yellow and Pink Bourbon are Bourbon sub-species.

CATIMOR, is a recent cross created in Portugal in 1959 to contrast some patho-gens that can cause damage to coffee plantations. Catimor derives form Caturra (an Arabica quality descending from Bourbon) and Timor, a natural hybrid of Arabica and Robusta that first appeared on the Indonesian island of the same name. From Canephora it takes its low acidity, high bitterness and limited aroma that at times can take on not very pleasing herby notes.

CATUAI, a varietal that was first introduced in Brazil in the 1950s, derives from a cross between Caturra and Mundo Novo. It is slightly more productive than Caturra and maintains a good level of bean quality.ntury. Compared to its par-ent, Caturra is shorter and has many more branches, qualitie

CATURRA, derives from a natural mutation of the Bourbon variety that was dis-covered in Brazil in the first half of the nineteenth century. Compared to its par-ent, Caturra is shorter and has many more branches, qualities that make it more productive and easier to handle.

COLOMBIA, a leaf-pathogen resistant hybrid created in the country of the same name.

GEISHA, or Gesha is a coffee quality named after the Ethiopian village from where it originated –Ghesa – a fact that not many are aware of, since nowadays the most famous (and expensive) Geisha coffee with its great sensorial properties mostly comes from Panama.

MARAGOGYPE is a mutation of Typica and is a shrub with a surprisingly rich foliage and large seeds.

MUNDO NOVO is one of the most cultivated coffee varieties in Brazil where it first originated in the 1940s by crossing Bourbon and Typica. Mundo Novo is known for its high yield.

PACAMARA is a Salvador hybrid (1958) generated by two Arabica coffee species, Pacas and Maragogype.

PACAS, is a natural mutation of Bourbon.

SL28 AND SL34 are varieties that were created in the 1930s in the Scott Laboratories in Kenya. These coffee plants grow fine and therefore expensive beans delivering a coffee with clear citrusy notes.

TIMOR is a natural hybrid of Arabica and Robusta that was selected on the island of Timor during the 1940s.

TYPICA, also known as Tipica, is one of the surviving original varietals. From Yemen it spread adapting to different climates, generating the Kona (Hawaii) and Blue Mountain (Jamaica) varietals. It has a limited yield but produces high quality coffee.

COFFEE – ITS TRAVELS THROUGH THE CENTURIES

Most historians agree in saying that the ancient province of Kaffa in southwestern Ethiopia was where coffee first originated perhaps around the early centuries of the last millennium. The first plantation was in Harar at 6000 feet (1885 meters) above sea level.

The reason why coffee took so long to make its way to the shelves of apothecaries and then later to become an everyday product is yet unknown, but what we do know is that its spread and success was determined by the physiologic effects caused by the beverage made from its fruits and seeds. Legend has it, these effects were first noticed by a shepherd who saw his goats become rather frisky after having eaten some coffee leaves from the plant (they too contain caffeine); but more likely, it was human curiosity that led someone in search of something new to eat to taste the coffee cherries. Whatever the case, coffee was hailed as one of nature's great gifts.

One of the many coffee posters Belgian artist Marc-Henri Meunier designed
for Rajan in 1899.

WHERE IS COFFEE CULTIVATED AND HOW

*Coffea Arabica leaves
and flowers.*

It is a fact that in the fourteenth century in Yemen there were coffee cultivations and the fruits were used to make a beverage capable of making people more alert, active and resistant to fatigue.

Over the two centuries that followed, coffee spread throughout the Middle East – almost on a par with the growth of Islam, a religion that having forbidden the consumption of alcoholic beverages found comfort in this invigorating drink that also took on a ritual significance through which this culture would differentiate itself from Christianity. Coffee then spread to India in the Mysore region, taken there by Baba Budan, a pilgrim who had smuggled seven raw coffee beans from Mecca.

During the seventeenth century, some Dutchmen got hold of a number of coffee seedlings which were planted in the botanical gardens of Amsterdam in order to be eventually transferred to the East Indies, where the Java and Sumatra plantations were initiated. In the early eighteenth century, French officer Gabriel de Clieu was entrusted with the task of transporting to Martinique one of the coffee seedlings that the Amsterdam Burgomaster had given as a gift to King Louis XIV. His mission succeeded marking the beginning of coffee plantations in the New World: only half a century later on the island there were almost twenty million plants. During those same years, the British decided that coffee shrub plantations might represent an excellent investment and began cultivations in Jamaica and India. The British were certainly not the only Europeans that decided to invest in coffee: France too extended its cultivations in Guyana, but unfortunately this nation was not as lucky. Legend has it that a certain Francisco de Melo Palheta had seduced the governor's wife who in 1727 gave him some coffee seedlings that he then took to Brazil, going down in history as the initiator of the world's largest coffee production.

In 1740 coffee arrived in Mexico, in 1784 it reached Venezuela, and around that same year it was in Colombia too. During the nineteenth century, African coffee cultivations increased greatly spreading to Congo and Madagascar, but also to Rwanda, Burundi and Tanganyika (a German East-Africa colony at the time) and in many other countries.

WHERE IS COFFEE CULTIVATED?

Coffee is cultivated in more than seventy-five countries around the world. Apart from only a few exceptions, all these countries lie in an area between the Tropic of Cancer and the Tropic of Capricorn. The origin of coffee beans matters, because it represents a discriminating factor on the market: consumers in fact can base their choice on origin, especially those who have travelled the world to taste all the different qualities, only to go back to enjoy the unsurpassed Italian Espresso blend, all the better when certified. In some cases, coffee origin corresponds to specific characteristics, because a certain territory is matched to specific climatic conditions, to certain species and varieties, and to certain processing methods of the raw beans. But in some cases origin is just a good way of trying out new coffee varieties.

Ask one hundred people returning from Brazil to describe the famous Brazilian Santos and you will probably get one hundred different answers. Because Santos is simply the name of the port where coffee is collected – coffee that has grown across a country that is as big as a continent, stretching 2730 miles from north to south and 2684 miles from east to west, and that therefore includes an extraordinary variety of coffees.

Being the world's largest coffee producer, Brazil is certainly the most prominent case, but the same is true for all other coffee producing countries of the equatorial belt. Coffee that is grouped by origin under the same name – Ethiopia, Colombia or India, you name it – necessarily includes a range of very different productions. Things change a bit when we refer to a relatively small area, or even to a single plantation (a finca) of one specific year. In this case, the combination of a single species, varietal, soil, and climate paired with a fixed set of cultural components are more likely to assure specific range of sensorial properties, provided that the roasting method remains constant without becoming a further variable.

Coffee plants require low heat and humidity conditions, so their cultivations can only be located in the so-called "coffee bean belt" between 22° North and 22° South. Different species, and also different soil conditions and cultivation methods within this same range can determine great differences in the productions across the various countries. Arabica loves the change of season and thrives in areas where temperatures range between 59 °F and 74 °F (15–23 °C). Robusta does not resist these temperature variations and prefers areas where it can always count on 75 °F to 85 °F (24–29 °C), such as the equatorial zone for instance (between 10° North and 10° South). Environmental conditions strongly influence coffee's sensorial properties. The first major differentiation is between high-altitude coffee and coffee grown at lower altitudes. Arabica plantations prefer areas between 2900 and 6500 feet (900–2000 meters) above sea level, whereas Robusta thrives between 650 and 1900 feet (200–600 meters) above sea level.

Conventionally, if the production area is around the equator, the line of demarcation for higher quality coffee is traced around 4900 feet (1500 meters), meaning that from this altitude the specific weight of the beans will be greater (the so-called hard beans, hence the denominations SHB Strictly Hard Beans, SHG Strictly High Grown, etcetera). The further down you go, the more the density of the beans will decrease (soft beans). Higher specific weight at high altitudes is a consequence of different climatic conditions combined with different sun exposure and thermal excursions which generate a higher concentration of fats, sugars and proteins in the seed (the future coffee bean). However, if the plantation is located near the tropics, the abovementioned conditions can already be found at relatively lower altitudes, even below 2900 feet (900 meters) above sea level.

Environmental conditions that allow the slow ripening of the fruit lead to a seed with a higher concentration of sugars, organic acids, amino acids and fats, which then generate aroma precursors that can be enhanced in the subsequent stages of the raw bean processing and roasting (such as for example, terpenes and diterpenes that generate floral aromas). Among the most significant factors influencing the final outcome is also social stability. A coffee plant takes years to develop and plantations require continuous maintenance: in the event of

A unique climate allows the cultivation of coffee on the hills of Manizales in Colombia.

social unrest, coffee plantations and processing plants cannot be managed suitably thereby negatively affecting the final product. Through recent coffee history, we can find many examples of coffee qualities that were once common and that have now become difficult to find, just think of the Yemen or Congo varietals.

In the future, however, we could be drinking types of coffee that are completely different from the ones we are used to now, without even knowing the reasons for this change. The situation is complex, but let's try to identify the key points. Climate change is causing temperatures to rise, and this could push Arabica towards higher grounds or to territories that are more distant from the equator, where it is cooler. This would avoid the destruction of plantations caused by pathogens that in warm climates spread with greater virulence, and against which these plants are defenseless. Unfortunately for Arabica there is no chance, in one case or the other. The only solution resides in creating resistant hybrids, which however would deprive Arabica of some characteristics that make it a favorite among coffee enthusiasts. Already 80% of the coffee grown in Colombia is of the Catimor variety, that is very resistant but characterized by rather persistent woody notes. In Brazil, there are new varieties of Robusta that could also grow in the Amazon, granting new territories to coffee cultivations, huge extensions with an average yield of over 15,000 lbs (7000 kilograms) of coffee per hectare, but delivering a product with little sensorial properties.

Another factor that must be considered is the emergence of new producer countries such as China, which already delivers on the market one million bags of coffee (over 132 million lbs, 60 million kilograms), and also the reduction of export rates of nations known for the high quality of their coffee, such as India and Mexico due to the increase in domestic consumption. It appears that higher living standards determine a rise in the consumption of coffee as opposed to other beverages, causing a further decrease of fine coffee on the market. Hope comes from improvements in African coffee production, especially Canephora coffee, provided new processing methods are adopted.

In fact, another factor that could lead to a noticeable change in the sensorial profile of coffee – especially espresso coffee, which is the most demanding brewing method – is determined by the drupes selection methods and raw beans treatment. A handpicked harvest assures that coffee cherries are picked only when ripe, but this method is practically disappearing. The result of this is that 80% of harvested fruits have a low percentage of sugar, while to make an excellent cup of coffee you need over-mature cherries with a high concentration of simple sugars. This is why the drupes should be carefully selected using different levels of quality for different purposes, not unlike what happens with grapes in the winemaking sector.

On the other hand, due to the significant impact of technology on the environment, the presence of washed coffee, with its fresh and fruity/floral aromas, is decreasing and the drying times of natural coffees are getting shorter – a trend that is highly detrimental to quality, since the endogen fermentation of the cherries cannot not occur, and the early killing of the germ stops the enzymatic activity responsible for the creation of aroma precursors. This is why in Brazil experimentations are being conducted with intermittent dryers that should allow a suitable development of the embryo before the deactivation of the germ.

After all these considerations, let us now look into the most important coffee origins (based on volume or on the contrary on rarity) or those that we are more likely to find inscribed on the packaging.

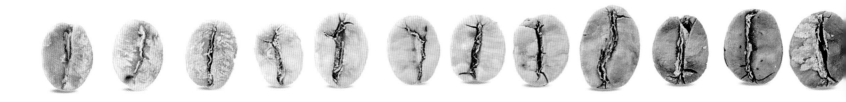

BRAZILIAN MOGIANA

Mogiana is one of the areas of the great Brazilian coffee qualities that are often grouped under the name of Santos, after the port from where Brazilian coffee has been traditionally exported. Located in the State of São Paulo on the border with Minas Gerais, this region is divided into three areas, Alta (High), Média (Mid) and Baixa (Low) Mogiana. The former two have been known for centuries for the quality of their coffee, a pure natural Arabica coffee, known for its good body, balanced acidity and distinct cocoa and chocolate notes in its aroma.

Mogiana Paulista has a mild climate with average temperatures around 68 °F (20 °C) and a yearly 5.5 feet (1700 millimeters) rainfall concentrated in spring and autumn, with no rain between May and September, that is the period of the coffee harvest that is followed by the drying of the drupes.

The sandy soil is red due to the high percentage of iron and lies at an altitude between 2400 and 3900 feet (750–1200 meters). Catuai and Mundo Novo varieties are the most common and the fruits are harvested from May to September, today more and more with powerful machines, a method that is facilitated by the gentle slopes and the geometric arrangement of the plantations. Either hand- or machine-picked, the cherries are then placed to dry on the ground according to the "dry" method (which we will describe shortly), well layered in the farmyards and turned over up to thirteen times a day to prevent abnormal fermentations. Ovens are also used but this method does not deliver the same result because it prevents the proper formation of enzymes.

CAMEROON ROBUSTA GG SUPERIOR

In this West African country, especially in the province of Ebolowa, the climate is relatively fresh with one rainy season from July to November. At around 2200 feet (700 meters) above sea level, on a kind of soil that is very similar to volcanic soil, grow cultivations of Robusta varietals originally from Zaire. The drupes are hand-picked one by one, from November to February and naturally processed to extract the beans. Once roasted, they deliver a coffee that very much retains the quality of its species: great body, low acidity, markedly bitter, toasted bread, cocoa, chocolate and the unmistakable ashy note. Nonetheless, it is one of the Robusta varietals with the cleanest taste.

COLOMBIA MEDELLIN SUPREMO

Contaminated in the nineteenth century by Venezuela with coffee that came from the French Antilles, over the last century Colombia became the world's second largest coffee producer and the world's leading washed-Arabica producer. In the Medellin region, at the foot of the Andes, at an altitude of around 5200 feet (1600 meters) above sea level, the coffee plantations thrive and flourish, growing one of the finest Colombian coffees.

The climate is subtropical, humid, relatively ventilated and with an average rainfall of 5.4 feet (1650 mm) and average annual temperatures around 72 °F (22 °C), with oscillations ranging from 61 °F to 99 °F (16–37 °C). The land is predominantly of volcanic origin and is home to many old and more recent varieties. The two harvests, between April and May followed by the principal one between October and December, are carried out by hand when the drupes are ripe. The yield is relatively low, delivering over 15000 lbs (7000 kilograms) per hectare. The green coffee bean processing is done following the "wet" method, removing the pulp from the drupes by letting them ferment and then later drying the seeds.

Although it is a washed coffee, Colombia Medellin Supremo has a good body and limited acidity with an aroma with notes of fresh fruit, chocolate, toasted bread, biscuits and walnut (a note that at times can become predominant).

COSTARICA SHB TARRAZU

Coffee was brought to Costa Rica from Cuba and the Antilles during the eighteenth century. Costa Rica proved particularly suited to the cultivation of this plant, with the region of Tarrazu (with its three subzones: San Marcos, San Lorenzo and San Carlos) delivering a produce of the highest quality.

The climate in this area has two seasons: the wet season (7.8 feet / 2400 mm average rainfall) from May to November and the dry season from December to April, with temperatures ranging between 63 °F and 83 °F (17–28 °C) with an average of around 66 °F (19 °C). The soil is of volcanic origin, rich in humus and minerals, and lies between 3900 feet (1200 meters) above sea level (therefore reaching the limit to obtain a Strictly Hard Bean) and 6200 feet (1900 meters) above sea level. Caturra and Catuai (strictly Arabica since Costa Rica has banned the cultivation of Robusta) are the most cultivated varieties that grow in the shade of tall trees delivering drupes which, harvested in the dry season, are removed of their pulp with the wet method and then dried in the open, in farm yards or on mats to obtain high density, shiny, flat, greenish-blue beans.

Correctly roasted this coffee variety translates into an interesting and elegant beverage, dry and slightly bitter, with a good acidity complemented by an aroma with clear notes of fresh, desiccated and dry fruit at times paired with hues of balsamic and spice.

ETHIOPIA YIRGACHEFFE

This is a prestigious coffee originally from the Gedeo zone surrounding the city of Yirgacheffe located at 6200 feet (1900 meters) above sea level. The Arabica plantations grow between 5500 and 8200 feet (1700–2500 meters) on a volcanic soil that is incredibly rich in minerals and where water drains away easily. In some cases, coffee plants coexist with tall trees, while in others they grow directly under the sun where temperatures are fresher thanks to altitude. The drupes are washed, therefore fermentation happens after the coffee fruit is pulped and dried (usually in the sun).

After roasting, Yirgacheffe delivers a thin body, sharp acidity coffee with an aroma of incredible complexity: plenty of tropical fruity citrusy notes (coconut and mandarin in the first place) ending with toasted bread, biscuit, chocolate, and in some cases, hazelnut.

ETHIOPIAN SIDAMO

This quality comes from the very birthplace of coffee, less than 100 miles (150 kilometers) from Kaffa, growing in the zone inhabited by the Sidama people.

The plantations are located at 5900 feet (1800 meters) above sea level on a fertile volcanic upland where temperatures range between 81 °F (27 °C) with rain mostly falling between February and April (1.9 to 6.5 feet/600–2000 mm per year). Drupes, pure Arabica in this area, ripen over a rather long period, between August and December and are generally hand-picked one by one and treated with the wet process method to obtain the fine small gray coffee beans. At the tasting this coffee reveals the typical elegant quality of washed coffees, thin body, no bitterness and a good level of acidity leading to a high level aroma: flowers, honey, citrus and tropical fruits, and then dry fruit that immediately leads to hues of light spices, at times followed by wild/animal scents adding depth and richness.

GUATEMALA ANTIGUA PASTORES

Guatemala Antigua Pastores plantations were introduced by the Jesuits in the eighteenth century and currently grow between 4900 and 5900 feet (1500–1800 meters above sea level), on slopes that were generated by volcanoes not far from Antigua, the city of knights of Guatemala that during the sixteenth century was the capital of the country.

Here on a volcanic soil made even more fertile by the large trees that populate the forests assuring fresh shade to the coffee plants, grow the ancient Bourbon and Typica varietals and the more recent Catuai. The drupes ripen between August and September and are still frequently handpicked and then of course pulped and fermented and then put to dry in the sun.

Among the coffees of Guatemala, Antigua Pastores is one of the finest: very malleable at the roasting, it maintains a good level of acidity that is complemented by a highly complex aroma where floral and fresh fruit notes combine with deeper toasted (bakery and cocoa) hues with touches of licorice and anise.

HAITIAN BLUE PINE FOREST

This quality comes from the southeastern region of the island of Haiti, Thiotte, the most renowned for the production of coffee. The average temperature is 77 °F (25 °C) with the dry season occurring between November and May, which is followed by the wet rainy season. The temperature excursion between day and night is remarkable and this leads to the formation of valuable precursors of aromas in the beans. The plantations, consisting largely of the Typica variety, grow on clay soils at altitudes of up to 5200 feet (1600 meters) above sea level. The drupes are worked with the wet system and roasted with great expertise, delivering a coffee that at the tasting displays clear pastry (caramel, biscuits) and dried fruit (especially almond) notes.

HAWAII KONA

There are five Hawaiian volcanoes and two of these (Hualalai and Mauna Loa) provide a soil that is particularly suitable to coffee cultivation, especially on the western side of the island where the climate is drier (rainfall is less that one foot, only a few hundred millimeters a year) and average temperatures around 77 °F (25 °C) with little fluctuations throughout the year. The lava that originated the soil is of the basaltic type and the Arabica plants grow in holes dug into the rock. The plants begin to flourish in February, with the first fruits ripening in August through to January of the following year. Once harvested, the coffee is treated with the wet method: after the drupes are pulped, the coffee is left to ferment for 36–48 hours, and then placed on the "hoshidana" covered drying decks for one or two weeks. After a careful roasting, the beans deliver an honest coffee, with clear and dominant fresh notes with a hint of aromatic herbs (mint can be appreciated at times) accompanied by more common notes of caramel and malt, dried fruit and sometimes pepper.

INDIAN MYSORE PLANTATION

Indian Mysore Plantation coffee has been cultivated since 1670 in the region of the same name in the southwestern part of the peninsula, in the area lying between the Kodagu mountain region and the Karnataka region. Rainfall in this area ranges between 5.7 and 7.2 feet (1750–2200 millimeters) – except for particular years in which it can reach 9.8 feet (3000 millimeters) – and is limited to July, August and November. The average temperature is 59 °F (15 °C), with minimum peaks of 52 °F (11 °C) and reaching maximum 83 °F (28 °C) between April and May. The coffee plantations are located at altitudes between 3200 and 4900 feet (1000–1500 meters) above sea level and for the most part consist of Cauvery coffee, which is a close relative of the Catimor, that is Arabica, growing in the shade of large trees. The drupe harvest takes place between October and February with a yield of about 6600 lbs (3000 kilograms) per hectare. The drupes are then treated with the wet system and, once dried, the beans are then selected. At the tasting, this coffee presents a thin body, with distinctive aromatic notes in the area of pastry and spices.

JAMAICAN BLUE MOUNTAIN

This coffee owes its name to the high Jamaican mountains that reach 8047 feet (2453 meters) above sea level. This region includes several micro-climate areas characterized by abundant rain (between 16 and 22 feet/ 5000 and 7000 mm a year) and fertile soils of volcanic origin, rich in nitrogen, phosphorus, potassium and an incredible variety of micro elements.

The name Blue Mountain identifies the Typica Arabica productions of the areas of St. Thomas, St. Andrew and Portland. This production is very slow and the drupes can take up to ten months to reach maturity. Hand-picked during the summer (until August) they are then treated with the wet method and later pulped, dried, fermented for a long period (even over a month) and left to dry with great care. This particular coffee is then stored and sold in white oak barrels, to distinguish it from all the other coffee-bean qualities typically placed in jute bags.

Blue Mountain is a very famous coffee and it has been written that this quality is the world's most complete. Although characterized by a certain acidity, when correctly roasted, it takes on a silky quality that highlights candied citrus fruit, almond, vanilla, chocolate and tobacco notes.

KENYA AA

On the terraced, acidic, volcanic soils around Mount Kenya, at altitudes ranging from 4200 and 6800 feet (1300–2100 meters) above sea level, grow Arabica plantations. Sheltered from the sun under tall banana trees, the coffee cherries ripen for the first harvest between June and August, followed by the main harvest occurring between October and December.
The skin and pulp of the fruit are removed with the wet method and the beans are then left to dry on cement flooring or simply on the ground on the farmyards.

Kenya coffee (AA indicates large size beans) is one of the world's most citrusy and floral coffees (sometimes even a note of rose can be detected). Markedly acid, this coffee bouquet is completed by notes of green apple and other fresh fruit.

KOPI LUWAK

In Java, Sumatra and Sulawesi lives a small mammal, an Asian palm civet that in Indonesia is known as Luwak (Paradoxurus hermaphroditus) that very much enjoys feeding on coffee drupes. This animal is known for being very choosy and only goes for the ripest fruits, from which it takes plenty of energy (the pulp can contain up to 25% of sugar), vitamins and minerals. Inside the animal's body, the chemical and biological reactions occurring in its gastrointestinal tract digest most of the drupe, but the seeds, rich in active olfactory molecules, are expelled in the feces. The local population collects the feces and then dries them in order to free and dry the beans that will then be used to produce one of the world's most expensive coffee qualities.

The abovementioned islands grow both Arabica and Robusta coffee, depending on the altitude of the plantation.

Made famous by its rarity, this coffee is slightly bitter with a very rich aroma, with clear dry fruit notes (hazelnut in many cases), pastry, spices with a hint of the substance in which the beans are collected. The quality of this coffee however is not always entirely worth its price, and the fact that today these mammals are raised and force-fed make the production of this coffee somewhat controversial.

MEXICO COATEPEC

This coffee comes from the Coatepec region of Mexico, characterized by a very rainy climate (6.2 feet/1900 millimeter average annual precipitation) especially between June and September, with temperatures ranging from 48 °F to 86 °F (9–30 °C). Plantations are located between 4200 and 4900 feet (1300–1500 meters) above sea level, growing on different kinds of soil, some richer in organic materials others richer in minerals. Among the main varietals of this region are two Arabica coffees, Typica and Flat. These highland coffee plants grow under large trees alongside many medicinal herbs, very useful for avoiding erosion. From November to January, the fruits are harvested. After being suitably selected, the beans are left to dry directly under the sun as prescribed by the dry method.

Duly roasted, these coffee beans deliver a natural coffee with great body, scarcely acid and with an aroma bouquet with notes of clear dry fruit, toasted bread, and chocolate, at times complemented by a touch of spice (pepper).

MEXICO MARAGOGYPE

In northern Chiapas, a dry region with temperatures oscillating between 59 °F and 95 °F (15–35 °C), at an altitude between 2600 and 4500 feet (800–1400 meters) above sea level, grows one of the coffee plants producing among the world's largest coffee beans: a variant of Typica, the Maragogype, an Arabica with seeds that can double and at times even triple the average size of a coffee bean.

Appreciated for its low caffeine content, this slightly bitter and fresh coffee has an aromatic bouquet with notes of apple, banana, honey, chocolate, tea and tobacco.

MONSOONED MALABAR

This coffee was born in India, growing in plantations growing between 3600 and 3900 feet (1100–1200 meters) above sea level, with average temperatures ranging between 77 °F and 83 °F (25–28 °C), and abundant rainfall (up to 6.5 feet/2.000 millimeters a year) between June and November. Here the Kent and Catuai drupes ripen between November and February. Once harvested and dried, the fruits are exposed to the monsoon winds for a period of three or four months: this is the factor that makes this coffee unique.

The idea of exposing the beans to the monsoon winds, which are particularly strong on the southwestern coast of India, came from the change that was noticed in the coffee beans that were transported from India to Europe, rounding the Cape of Good Hope. Not only did those beans change color passing from green to yellow, but when roasted they displayed a greater balance matched with a particularly captivating aroma. The process was thus replicated on dry land by exposing the beans to the very damp winds that blow on the Malabar coast.

The Monsooned Malabar, especially when used to make espresso coffee, reveals a rich body enhanced by low acidity and a great aroma mainly characterized by notes of dry fruit, chocolate and spices. In some cases however, when fermentation is not completely successful, there are musty notes reminiscent of dairy products.

NEPAL MOUNT EVEREST SUPREME

Not only is Mount Everest the highest mountain in the world, it is also one of the few places north of the Tropic of Cancer where coffee cherries ripen. Here, in the Nuwakot region, at the foot of the Ganesh Imal mountains, there is a monsoon climate area with rain and wind from June to August, at over 6500–7800 feet (2000–2400 meters) above sea level: here grow the Caturra Arabica plantations that between November and January deliver ripe dark red drupes rich in aromatic compounds. Treated with the wet method, the beans are then skillfully roasted producing a round-tasting bitter coffee, with low-level acidity, and a very rich aromatic bouquet with a play of notes of citrus, ginger, cinnamon, cocoa, tobacco and almond. For these qualities Nepal Mount Everest Supreme is known as the meditation coffee.

PUERTO RICO YAUCO SELECTO

This coffee grows in the Caribbean, on the smallest island of the Greater Antilles: Puerto Rico, where coffee arrived in 1736 from Martinique. The city of Yauco was founded thirty years later, shortly becoming the city of coffee par excellence.

The plantations are exposed to the long rain season (from October to February) and grow on the mostly volcanic fertile soil. Once ripe, the Bourbon drupes are harvested by hand, treated with the wet process, and then left to dry in the sun.

If Puerto Rico coffee is already a prized quality in itself, the Puerto Rico Yauco Selecto, which represents only 1% of the overall island production, is even more exclusive. If correctly roasted, this coffee is definitely worth its price, awarding coffee enthusiasts with its rich body, great freshness, very little bitterness and an aromatic bouquet of great depth: dry and fresh fruit, cereals and pastry, sometimes with a not too subtle hint of peanut.

SAINT HELENA

Saint Helena is one of the world's most exclusive coffees. It grows on the famous island of the same name in the middle of the Ocean, half way between Africa and America where Napoleon was sent in exile. Its climate, although subtropical, is unique: reached by the Trade Winds, the island's temperatures on the coast range between 58 °F and 90 °F (14–32 °C) and fall further inland, with a relatively low yearly rainfall up to a maximum 3.2 feet (1000 mm).

The plantations consisting of Bourbon plants, grow at an altitude of about 2200 feet (700 meters) above sea level on the rich volcanic soil, made even richer by guano – bird excrements. Tall trees protect the Coffea Arabica shrubs from the sun and the winds. The yield of these plants is however very low. Drupes are harvested twice a year. Treated with the wet method, they are then left to dry for a long time, several months even. The result is extraordinary, so much so that there are coffee tasters who affirm that Saint Helena is the world's best coffee. Its sensorial properties include good acidity complemented by floral and fruity notes with interesting citrusy hues, followed by toasted bread, pastries and dried fruit.

GIANT SALVADOR PACAMARA

Maragogype, the extraordinary varietal of the Bourbon that developed in Brazil, in the small state of El Salvador on the Pacific Ocean generated the Pacamara that like its parent has incredibly large beans. Here, on the fertile soil of this country's volcanic mountain range well irrigated by rains (over 6.5 feet/2000 millimeters yearly rainfall) between May and October, the Pacamara carries out its cycle that leads to the ripening of the fruits between January and May. The yield per hectare is rather low, but the result in the cup is truly satisfying with a very balanced cup quality with fresh and surprising herby notes (tea and tobacco), complemented by touches of spice (licorice) and toasted pastry.

SULAWESI KOPI TORAJA TONGKONAN

The island of Sulawesi is located in Indonesia and enjoys a tropical climate, with an average temperature of 86 °F (30 °C) year-round, with a dry season from May to August and a rainy season from November to March. The territory is mountainous, therefore there are several different internal microclimates. The coffee plantations grow at altitudes ranging between 4200 and 6500 feet (1300–2000 meters) above sea level, on volcanic soil (some volcanoes on the island are still active) and therefore very rich in precious minerals beneficial to the coffee plants that grow protected by tall trees. The variety cultivated on the island is Jember, or Kopy Jember, also known as S795, a hybrid derived from a natural crossing of Arabica and Liberica with Kent. This variety has a very scarce yield (3300 lbs/1500 kilograms per hectare), and its plants can reach a height of 19 feet (6 meters) and can live up to fifty years.

Also interesting is the traditional coffee processing method adopted for this variety: a wet method, with the variant that the drupes are left to ferment in small containers (barrels) and then dried over long periods (even up to a month) due to the difficult weather conditions. The final outcome is one of the world's most exclusive coffees, due to its limited production, its accurate selection process, its particular storage in small barrels and for its unique sensorial properties: although washed, this coffee has good body and moderate acidity, as well as an aromatic bouquet with accents of balsamic notes and spices combined with fresh and dried fruit.

WHERE IS COFFEE CULTIVATED AND HOW

HOW IS COFFEE CULTIVATED?

The propagation of the coffee plant can take place by sowing or cutting. The first method entails collecting ripe fruits, selecting the best seeds and putting them in wooden boxes covered with earth and humus waiting for the new seedlings to grow. With the second method, instead you take a branch from a fully-grown plant and then plant it in the soil. Placed in what is called a nursery, the future coffee plants remain there for about one year to be later transferred to the actual plantations where, after about three years, they will begin to produce. As you can see, the coffee plant is not very different from vine in terms of planting and fructification timing, and the same goes for the plant's duration: on average, a coffee plantation is productive for about twenty years. But of course there are variations and exceptions: in some areas coffee plants can live for half a century and there are even single plants that have lived over a century.

The choice between using the seed or the cutting method for propagation depends on the objectives: the first method is certainly more practical, the second guarantees that the new seedlings will maintain the same characteristics of their parent. In fact, it is impossible to know for certain the contamination and the combination of genes that will descend from the fertilized flower: that is how mutations and hybrids are born, either naturally or by human intervention.

A coffee plantation inspection in the
Orosi River Valley in Costa Rica.

THE PLANTATION

The environments for the cultivation of coffee can be very different in terms of orography (land elevations, slopes, etc.), type of soil (from volcanic to the red Brazilian lands), rainfall, and wind and sun exposure. Coffee plants can also grow under tall shady trees or even under direct sunlight. Another factor associated with the environment is the virulence of the plants' enemies, parasites that can compromise a plantation's production and even its very existence. The set of environmental characteristics of a specific area strongly affects the choice of an appropriate coffee species and variety, and the adoption of particular cultivation techniques.

In terms of soil, coffee plants prefer light, well-drained soils, rich in humus, nitrogen, potassium and phosphorus. Nitrogen is the main element in the growth of trunk and leaves, potassium is the basic agent in the production of drupes rich in sugar (important: the higher the concentration of sugars the greater the aroma of the roasted beans), while phosphorus is essential for flowering and therefore for the production of the drupes. It is also known that coffee plants love the shade, although light is the primary source of energy for the synthesis of cellulose and therefore for their growth. This is why exposure – which is also connected to windiness, transpiration and pollination – is also very important.

Equally important is annual rainfall in terms of quantity and distribution. If, on the one hand, superior plants that live beyond the tropics base their cycle on the seasons (the change of temperature and sun exposure), on the other hand coffee plants base their cycle on rain, blooming after every rainfall.

The incredible geometries of a Brazilian plantation.

WHERE IS COFFEE CULTIVATED AND HOW

WHERE IS COFFEE CULTIVATED AND HOW

Also relevant in terms of climate is the extraordinary interaction between latitude and altitude. Moving away from the equator the average temperature drops and generally the slopes are less steep: take for example the Brazilian hills of Mogiana and Minas where coffee plants grow at low altitudes (Arabica around 1600 feet/500 meters above sea level), directly under the sun, in low orderly rows, as if they were vineyards. These conditions permit mechanical harvesting, but the scarcity of water does not allow the production of washed coffees that require adoption of the "wet" method. On the contrary, closer to the equator, temperatures are higher and therefore, to find the right climate, coffee must find higher grounds even up to 9100 feet (2800 meters) above sea level. In these areas the sun is too strong and therefore the coffee plants must grow in the shade of tall trees on steep slopes and uneven soils, conditions that make mechanical harvesting impossible. But on the other hand there is plenty of water that allows the production of exclusive washed coffee. The altitude also affects to some extent the density of the drupes, an aspect that is strongly related to the fruit's degree of sugar and which has led to the distinction between hard beans and soft beans. The demarcation line between the two typologies is conventionally set at about 4900 feet (1500 meters) above sea level, but as we said before, the definition of this limit is strongly conditioned by latitude, exposition, type of plantation, and of course species and varietal.

Another key factor in defining the quality of a type of coffee is thermal excursion (that is the temperature difference between day and night). Thermal excursion affects the formation of terpenic precursors that determine the coffee's capacity to deliver floral and balsamic hints in the cup. This particular feature that is more commonly found in high-altitude washed coffees, is also interestingly present in certain natural coffees

Rows of coffee trees on the Hawaiian island of Kauai.

(that is coffees treated with the dry method) that grow at lower altitudes in regions that especially in the period of drupe ripening experience a high temperature excursion.

Finally, environmental conditions have a significant influence on the production of caffeine and phenolic acids. Caffeine is the alkaloid that gives coffee its much-loved psychotropic properties, but that can also limit the consumption of the beverage if in high concentration. Simply put: if coffee must be a pleasure, and if the levels of caffeine are high, then coffee should be consumed with moderation. Phenolic acids are common to all vegetables, but when they surpass certain levels or when they are of specific types, they become too present creating a rather unpleasant effect called astringency (unripe persimmon).

Caffeine and phenolic acids are important defenses for the plant, therefore if coffee is cultivated in conditions where it does not need to defend itself, from parasites for example, the plant will have less of these molecules. Elevation, for instance, lowers the risks of such menaces, and therefore Robusta coffee that grows on higher grounds is a bit less "Robusta" and the Arabica cultivated at lower altitudes is a bit more "Robusta."

LIFE CYCLE OF THE COFFEE PLANT

At our latitudes plants flower in spring, that is when temperatures rise announcing the end of winter. In tropical countries, what determines the flowering is the rain.

After each rainfall, the coffee plant grows its small white flowers that once pollinated produce what botanists call drupes, the fruits commonly known as cherries. The environment in which the plant lives might have one wet and one dry season, or it might be characterized by one single season with intermittent rain and dry weather. In this latter circumstance, the same plant will contemporarily present flowers, recently pollinated fruits, ripening drupes, and cherries ripe for the picking. That is why, unlike the grape harvest that is concentrated in a couple of months at most, we find regions where the coffee harvest can last throughout most of the year, or where there are two harvests in the same year. This means that the length of the period between the pollination of the flower and the ripening of the drupe can vary significantly – being anywhere in between six and ten months – depending on the zone.

In any case, after pollination, the ovary begins to grow, and the drupe forms. Green at first, it then turns bright red and then almost brown. But there are cases of orange drupes. It depends on the quality, just as it is with grapes.

THE FRUIT

The fruit of the coffee is a drupe and therefore fleshy, with thin exocarp (skin), juicy and sugary sarcocarp (pulp), fine and fibrous endocarp (parchment), a silvery film, and finally two seeds with the flat sides pressed against each other. The seeds are generally two, but sometimes, due to the abortion of one of the two, all the space is occupied by a single bean that delivers a very particular type of coffee known as "caracolito".

Different seeds identify different species: Arabica beans have an S-shape crack down the middle of the flat side, while Robusta beans have a straight line. Robusta seeds are generally smaller and rounder, while Arabica are larger and more elliptical in shape.

Smaller compared to the best-known drupes such as cherries, and despite its abundance of sugars and organic acids, coffee drupes are not used and, indeed, often represent a cost in environmental terms. What matters to humans are the two seeds, only measuring a few millimeters in certain species, ovzer one centimeter in others such as the Maragogype. It takes about fifty beans to make one cup of coffee, but since the Coffea shrubs are not grown in our gardens, let's see how they are turned into coffee.

48-49 Red coffee drupes in Brazil.

50-51 Coffee harvest in Zambia.

WHERE IS COFFEE CULTIVATED AND HOW

HARVESTING TECHNIQUES: PICKING, STRIPPING, AND MECHANICAL HARVESTING

Once ripe, the fruit is detached from the plant. There are three different ways this task can be carried out. The first one is called coffee picking and consists in picking the drupes one by one, as if they were cherries. Although the peel of the coffee fruit is very resistant, it nonetheless can be damaged causing the fruit to start to rot, a circumstance that might give the beverage rather unpleasant putrid notes, not unlike those one might smell next to a pile of garbage. The riper the fruit the more delicate it becomes, therefore the over-ripe fruits necessary to obtain some particular coffees of the highest quality are extremely delicate. In this case, manual coffee picking is the best method, but by far the most expensive.

A less expensive manual method is stripping: the coffee branch is held with one hand and with the other it is stripped of all its drupes, making them fall into containers (aprons, baskets or other) placed below them.

52-53 On this plantation in Thailand, ripe coffee drupes are handpicked one by one.

54-55 A great harvest at a coffee plantation in Ethiopia.

This method is fast, but with the drupes it also collects many leaves and, most importantly, it is impossible to make a distinction between the different levels of ripeness. Therefore this method can only be used on those varieties growing in areas where the fruits ripen all at the same time.

The last method is mechanical harvesting: large machines pass over the plantation rows, whipping the coffee plants in order to make the fruit fall into a hopper. This method of course can only be used where the land and the shape of the plantation allow it, such as in large plantations and in *fazendas* where there can be a selection of the beans based on their level of ripeness.

Regardless of the method, the level of ripeness of the beans is crucial for three reasons:

- ripe fruits have less phenolic acids that cause astringency and less malic acid whose effect is not reduced by roasting giving the beverage a rather unpleasant hardness in terms of flavor;

- ripening also reduces levels of pyrazine that are responsible for bold herby notes and ashy flavor once the beans are roasted;

- in ripe drupes, the concertation of sugars can reach 23/25%, a condition that is essential in order to obtain a significant aromatic intensity with the roasting.

THE EXTRACTION OF THE BEANS

Although the coffee drupe does not have much of pulp, the latter nonetheless represents a good percentage of the overall fruit and has to be removed along with the skin, in order to get to the coffee beans.

The oldest method, known as the "dry" method delivering the so-called "natural" coffees, simply lets the sun do all the work: the drupes are placed onto the farmyard ground (nowadays the ground is usually tiled in order to avoid unwanted contaminations affecting the final result). Here the drupes are left to dry gradually losing their moisture. The pulp and the skin lose elasticity, become dry and can be easily removed, leaving the coffee bean still wrapped in its chaff (silver-skin).

The conditions under which this transformation takes place – above all its duration – are very important for the development of the aroma precursors, which will eventually emerge during the roasting phase and in the final beverage. Natural coffees are necessary to obtain a coffee that has good body and low acidity, with hints of chocolate and sometimes spices, pepper in particular.

57 Coffee drying in the sun in Nicaragua.

*58-59 Thanks to meticulous and incessant work, the coffee harvest of this southern
Indian plantation can be left to dry in the sun.*

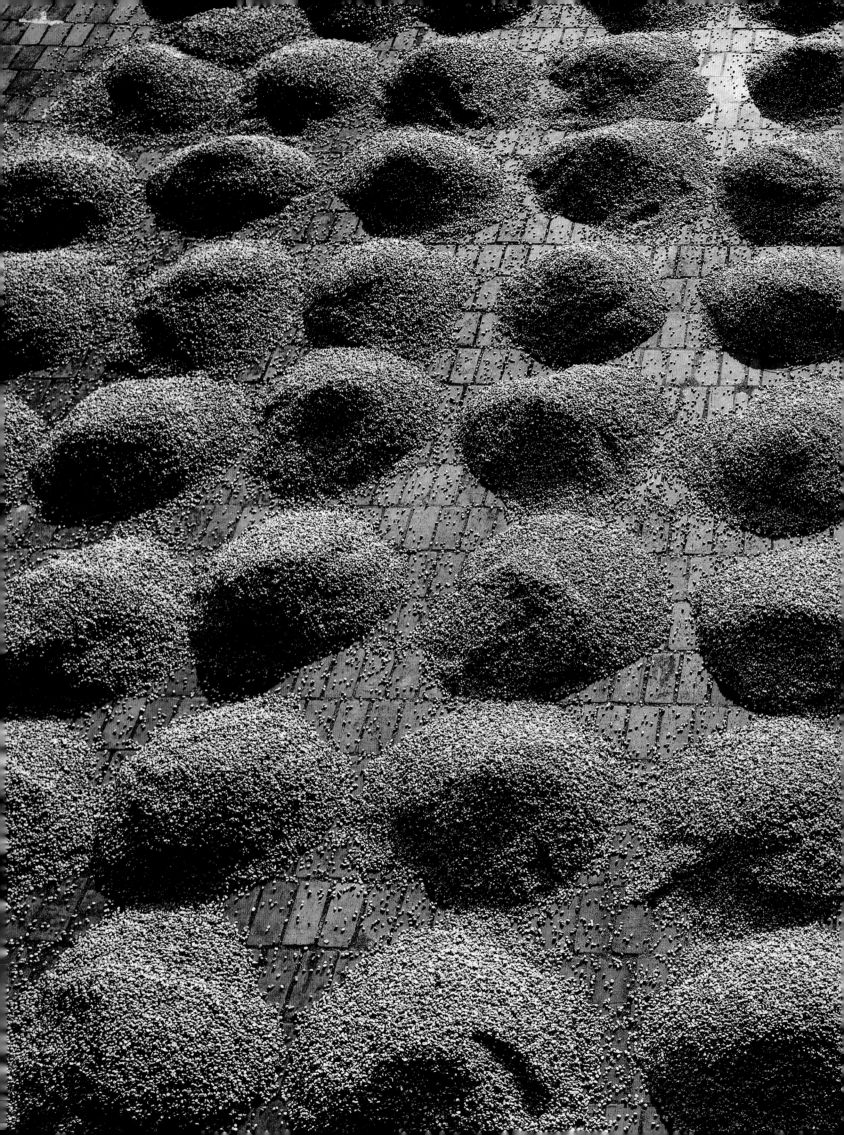

Although the process does not enhance the floral notes, when the coffee comes from environments with strong temperature variations there can be traces of floral, as well as elegant balsamic notes, that have nothing to do with the coarse green notes of unripe beans.

The second method is the so-called "wet processing" that delivers the "washed coffees". Although the traditional wet method is still adopted in small areas, this technique is more modern, because it requires machines capable of removing peel and pulp in order to leave the beans simply wrapped in a sugary, sticky film. Originally this operation was carried out with mortars and pestles, then over the years more and more efficient machines were introduced. The coffee beans are separated from their outer layers by placing the fruit into the water to ferment. In the water starts the generally spontaneous and therefore hard to control action of armies microorganisms (mostly yeasts and bacteria; molds are hindered by rather high levels of acidity). These microorganisms feed on the residual sugars, and produce strong amounts of enzymes that attack the outer layers leaving only the beans, which are then ready to be dried in the sun or in the shade, often on mats kept at a reasonable distance from the ground, placed in thin layers and continually turned over, moved around, and covered at night. In some cases, these driers have a roof to protect the beans from direct sunlight.

Guatemala: coffee drupes being washed to separate the precious seeds from the pulp.

WHERE IS COFFEE CULTIVATED AND HOW

Washed coffees can only be produced in areas where there is plenty of water and low-cost work force, because generally this type of process is reserved for drupes collected with the picking method. However, wet-processed beans produce fine coffee qualities since they deliver fresh acid notes, they are scarcely bitter, never astringent and cover a wide aromatic spectrum: honey, flowers (even rose notes), tropical fruit, citrus and stone fruit (such as peach and apricot), and dried fruit, walnut especially.

The third method is quite recent and delivers the semi-washed coffees. This procedure has been in use since the pulping machines have reached such high levels of efficiency that they clean the grains perfectly and making them ready for drying. The beans treated with this method provide coffee with intermediate characteristics between those obtained with the two older processes, but in reality, they have little in common with the fully-washed coffees, not having been through the fermentation process.

In the preparation of green coffee (this is how coffee is called before being roasted) it must be considered that the producers' main aim is usually that of a safe and steady production. A goal that has been definitely achieved, sometimes at the expense of high quality results. In short: all (most) coffees are good, none (almost none), are excellent. An important tool towards this objective is the drying oven that certainly avoids dangerous fermentations, but abbreviates the process to the point that the bean does not go through the de-structuring of important elements and there is not the time for the forming of precious enzymes. The drying oven also makes it unnecessary for the beans to lie in the sun whose action experts believe plays an important role in the formation of aroma precursors.

SELECTION, CLASSIFICATION AND PACKAGING

Depending on the general quality level of a production, the drupes undergo a more or less thorough selection. But when it comes to beans, selection is crucial. The bean selection can be carried out manually by workers who cannot endure heavy labor (usually youths, women and the elderly) or by machines that read the color of the beans that pass one by one in front of a light beam. This operation aims to eliminate any defected beans in order to comply with product classification standards. But with the advent of mechanical harvesting, the selection process has become even more important in order to avoid the presence of unripe beans, that can strongly compromise the quality of the brewed coffee. Another classification is based on the size of the beans that are sorted by sifting them through punched screens with specifically sized holes. The most valuable coffee beans reach screen 17/18, while the smaller ones are considered less valuable, even though this is not always the case as far as sensorial properties are concerned. Nonetheless, batches of coffee beans that are all the same size assure a significantly better roasting process.

Cupping, the sensory evaluation of coffee, is equally important: in the areas where coffee is produced there are professional coffee tasters who can taste up to 300 coffees a day, all prepared with the Brazilian method, that is infusing ground coffee in hot water. This method works for the tasting process, but it is not enough for some specific coffee preparations, such as Italian espresso coffee. Once selected and classified, the coffee is ready for packaging. The beans are usually stored in 132 lbs (60 kg) jute bags (there are very few exceptions to this size), often printed with the name of the producer and/or the origin of the coffee, or in other more voluminous containers or, alternatively, small wooden barrels for coffee qualities that need to declare their value.

64-65 Workers controlling and selecting coffee drupes on a southern Indian plantation.

ROASTING

FROM PERFORATED ROASTING PANS TO FLUID BED ROASTERS

Humankind's discovery of fire not only had an effect on the hygienic characteristics of food, but also on its sensory characteristics increasing pleasure. This discovery soon affected the consumption of coffee that passed from the boiling of drupes to the infusion of skillfully roasted beans.

Although the coffee drupes have, as we have already seen, a sugary pulp, humans have never liked them very much. Unlike other fruits, they do not have a captivating aroma – the green note is predominant and is generally persistent and coarse – and in the mouth, sweetness is offset by marked acidity, often combined with astringency. A decoction of coffee drupes was probably nothing special, and had humankind stopped at that, probably coffee would have not become so popular.

Even the raw beans taste herby (they are in fact called green-coffee) but if duly roasted they produce a highly attractive scent, and there have been some who have affirmed that a cup of brewed coffee contains twice as many molecules than there are in wine. That might be stretching it too far, but certainly roasting dramatically increases these molecules, to the point that in the final product there can be over 1500 of them. And these are the ones we have been able to count today. Who knows how many we will be able to identify in the future with the advancement of technology. And our sense of smell can detect some notes that technical equipment cannot identify and some can have a subliminal attraction.

Perhaps it was the molecules that reached the nostrils of our ancestors during a fire that spread among some coffee plants; perhaps, more likely, coffee was just another ingredient man experimented with after the discovery of fire. We will never know. But what we do know is that the discovery of roasted coffee beans left a mark on the course of history, dividing for centuries humankind into two great cultures: one that drank fermented drinks (wine and beer) and one that relied on the invigorating power of coffee.

We do not know what the first roasting equipment was like, but it probably was a terracotta vessel. But baked clay, or its most noble form ceramic, are not good heat conductors, unlike metal, whose discovery probably came before that of roasted coffee. Whether terracotta or metal, we can posit these early roasting vessels had holes in them leaving a certain level of contact between the flame and the beans. So probably, in the mouth of the ancient taster coffee had notes of roasted chestnut. So that was the origin of the perforated roasting pan that is still used today. Some old roasting pans were basically just a pan with the later addition of a lid with a handle to keep the beans moving over the heat.

In this case – and until the end of the nineteenth century – roasting took place by conduction, that is to say by supplying heat through a material such as iron.

The goal was achieved, but often the aroma was altered by empyreumatic hints and the taste affected by a not very pleasant contrast of bitter and sour. The use of hollow steel spheres rotating over a source of heat, usually burning wood, improved the roasting result assuring greater homogeneity. Wood was eventually replaced by coal that could be controlled better thereby contributing to some extent to further innovations. The real leap in quality came after World War II with the introduction of gas-heated roasters where heat conduction was entrusted to hot air.

We will get there shortly, because we need to consider two other aspects that have made the roasting process so critical: smoke and cooling. When roasting coffee there will always be smoke besides of course that generated by the source of heat. At the beginning of the last century, when professional coffee roasters were founded processing great quantities of produce, smoke extractors were installed to convey smoke outside.

Almost at the same time, remedies had to be found to avoid the slow cooling of the beans. When coffee beans reach a certain cooking point they start to emit heat rather than absorbing it. This causes the bean to continue roasting even when it is removed from the heat, a circumstance that can seriously compromise quality, especially if there are great quantities of coffee beans being roasted. In home roasting – today still practiced in some countries, such as Japan for instance, where green coffee is sold as a market grocery – the quantities are of course much smaller and it is sufficient to place the beans on a cold surface to stop their roasting. In early roasting establishments, the beans were discharged onto static grids raised from the ground, where the beans were turned over and over again as quickly as possible to make them cool down. Then the forced air cooling basins were invented. The latest invention to cool down the beans is a technique that uses nitrogen due to its capacity to freeze the air. Alongside these effective processes, there have been those who thought of doing things the quick way by spraying the roasted beans with some water to cool them: certainly the best way to ruin the coffee's aroma and shorten its life.

But let's go back to the roasting techniques: wood – which is still used in Brazil and by some artisans all over the world – was in some cases replaced by coal, then diesel, and then gas. Roasting was therefore no longer carried out by conduction, but by convection, with a major impact on the final product. From this point of view, it is impossible not to mention an innovation that occurred over the last quarter of the century: the use of clean air for the channeling of heat.

But innovation did not stop at drum coffee roasters. Coffee beans have even been roasted through irradiation (the microwave, that is), in Archimedean screw-pump machines that push coffee beans into a current of hot air, and even in fluid bed roasters where green beans are dropped into a high temperature air cyclone. During their fall the beans bake, lose weight, float and then are expelled from the top.

ROASTING TECHNIQUES

For a long time roasters were all built in the same way: a rotating cylinder containing coffee beans hit by hot air. These drum roasters lasted centuries, were used for a lifetime and more and have capacities ranging from a few to hundreds of pounds. Professionals say the best ones are the 132 to 264 lbs (60–120 kilogram) roasters, but excellent coffees can be roasted even in 33 or 771 lbs (15 and 350 kg) machines. Large scale processing however can be a hazard, and very small quantities also follow rules of their own.

But ultimately the Italian Espresso coffee, considered by everyone as the most demanding preparation, is based on coffee that was roasted in drum machines of this type that worked in "cooking batches" (consisting of a loading phase, a toasting phase and a discharge) with cycles varying between 15 and 25 minutes, that is the time necessary for a full formation of the aromas, and at temperatures ranging between 185 °F and 419 °F (85–215 °C). Nowadays there are roasters with sophisticated software that makes the process safer, but they must always be kept in check in order to obtain the best roasted beans.

From what has been said so far, it is easy to see how the first fundamental choice is precisely the selection of the green coffee that will be used: a very complex, difficult, and risky choice. An intuitive choice,

Coffee beans being roasted.

70 and 71 Four different levels of roasting.

still mostly based on the professional's sense of smell and experience, and that is taken by placing a certain amount of coffee into drum roasters (with capacities ranging between 0.2 to 2.2 lbs / 100 grams to one kilo) and bringing it to the desired level of roasting. This is the first step that can translate into a fatal mistake: usually small-scale roasting never delivers the result that will be obtained on an industrial scale. As we will see, heat produced by the mass of coffee, especially in the passage from the endothermic phase to the exothermic phase is related to the size of the mass itself, but not in a linear way.

WHAT HAPPENS DURING THE ROASTING PROCESS

Inside the roaster the beans receive heat and become a chemical reactor of their own constituents. In a first phase (endothermic phase) the bean receives heat from the outside that is spread within the bean by conduction, based on the transport of water vapor and carbon dioxide. In the second phase (exothermic phase), the bean's own constituents begin to produce heat, developing what is in fact a process of combustion that would ultimately lead to the destruction of the coffee if it were not stopped in time.

In more detail, in the endothermic phase during which the grain is a heat acceptor, the bean loses water and begins to change color, turning from green to pale yellow, while the scent passes from green to that of baked bread. That is when the hydrolysis of the sugars begins, initiating the Maillard reaction, the most important reaction of the roasting process. Subsequently the coffee reaches its first endothermic peak. The color becomes even more intense and the beans begin to inflate due to internal gas formation. Very soon, the exothermic reaction kicks in, with a strong increase in volume and the formation of micro-pores and superficial micro-cracks. The beans become fragile and a powerful aroma develops. The pyrolytic reactions become stronger and the grain begins to release large quantities of gas, while the coffee beans take on their final character.

Out of the roaster come completely transformed coffee beans, from a physical and chemical point of view. They have lost elasticity and have grown in volume by about 60%, their humidity is reduced by nine tenths, their sugar content is five times lower and, in the unwashed coffee beans, where weight loss amounts to 20%, there are higher levels of fats and nitrogen compounds. The real miracle, however, lies in the fact that through roasting these beans each transform into a treasure chest filled with aromas encased in an atmosphere of carbon dioxide.

72-73 Roasted coffee being cooled.

Through roasting, the basic constituents of the beans have created new chemical compounds. By reacting to each other, they form new ones that then go on to forming a third generation of elements and in some cases even a fourth and a fifth. So what might be a slight difference in the green coffee beans will be greatly amplified through roasting; what might be a small imperfection can turn out to be a catastrophe on the final sensory level.

ROASTING METHODS

If we place time and temperature – the two elements that allow us to regulate the energy required to roast coffee – on a four-quadrant diagram we can visualize four different situations:

- fast high-temperature roasting: can deliver uneven cooking of the beans that can be carbonized on the outside and poorly cooked on the inside. In terms of sensorial properties, when coffee is prepared using the espresso method, it has no cream (there is little of it and it is not persistent, with lack of texture), there is no harmony between bitterness and acidity (both strong), lack of body with tendency to astringency, empyreumatic scents and little aroma complexity;

- long high-temperature roasting: delivers a dark roast. The color of the cream becomes more intense, the astringent factor tends to become more pronounced, and so does bitterness. Floral and fruity notes disappear and, due to the increase in the formation of phenols, medicinal notes surface too. The vinylguaiacol and ethyl-guaiacol ratio inverts in favor of the former, with a reduction in the aromatic fineness;

- long low-temperature roasting: this combination produces an excessive formation of particular molecules called pyridines which give a more bitter taste and hints of cooked meat, but also increases the production of thiophene which, beyond a certain limit, rather than producing notes of honey, flowers and toasted bread, turns to an oniony scent.

- short low-temperature roasting: light roast. When light roast coffee is used for espresso, the result has little cream and texture, and lacks macromolecules (especially due to the fact that proteins and sugars do not blend), and for the same reason the body is thin. The acidity is high due to the reduced degradation of fixed aliphatic acids and this further contributes to disharmony in the cup, but above all the aroma is poor because there has not been an adequate formation of aromatic molecules.

REST TIME – DEGASSING

The freshly roasted bean cannot be used straight away and must be left to rest for some time in order to de-gas, that is to lose the excess gas within it while it continues its aromatic evolution. This operation is heavily affected by environmental conditions since temperature and pressure in the degassing environment accelerate or slow down the process. This procedure can be carried out in a variety of ways. In medium-sized coffee roasters it is common to use silos in which the roasted coffee is kept for a few days before being packaged.

In other cases, the beans are packed almost immediately letting them rest inside the bags, especially if that coffee is for export and must travel long distances. Regardless of the method, degassing is a necessary step: the freshly roasted coffee beans produce a cream that is extremely rich in carbon dioxide with a spongy appearance and little persistence. Moreover, from an olfactory point of view, freshly roasted coffee beans have little aroma because their aromatic development is not complete. Of course the beans must not be over-degassed in order to avoid the oxidation of the product.

SINGLE-ORIGIN COFFEES AND BLENDS

A good share of the 700 billion cups of coffee that are consumed around the planet each year are made from single-origin coffees – coffees from a territory that can be either as large as Brazil or correspond to one single plantation. As we have said before, in the first case, it doesn't really make much sense to talk about a single origin, while in the second the coffees could even be divided by year of production. As for wine, single-origin coffee bases its identity on its supposed or established peculiarities that if processed by a micro-roasting establishment, can translate into legendary specialties. On the other hand, when we speak of single-origin coffee from vast territories, the product still has an evocative power, but its characteristics are not so defined, since different batches will be mixed together to deliver the final product. The result is in fact a blend, but not as we commonly understand it.

In a world that celebrates the single-origin coffees, coffee blends are the only answer to our ancestral need for aromatic complexity. Commercially speaking, a blend is the coffee roaster's signature: if the origins of the different coffees can be very similar, the roasting process and the combination of the different coffees express the roaster's personality identifying his brand.

On the international markets, the ability to create good blends is a skill that is still nowadays associated with Italian tradition and expertise, generating great curiosity among non-Italian professionals. In fact, an exclusive blend cannot be created by simply applying a set of rules, but is rather an expression of a vision, almost an anthropological vision we could say, of how different coffees can harmoniously combine into a single cup. It is no coincidence that the first blends were made for Italian Espresso coffee (the earliest record of this method dates from 1845), a preparation that more than any other highlights in the cup the quality of green coffee and the skill of the roaster.

There are many types of coffee. Different coffee origins can be roasted separately and then mixed according to a precise recipe. Alternatively, green coffee beans can be mixed beforehand and then roasted.

Here follow the characteristics that a great blend should have to make a great cup of coffee:

- perfection: absence of any visual defects (no defects in the cream), no unpleasant scents and flavors and perfect balance in the mouth with no trace of astringency. The absence of flaws is matched by the following qualities: hazelnut color with tawny nuances in the cream, silkiness on the palate, perfect balance between acid and bitterness, fine and clear fragrance;

- depth: a quality that is mainly related to aroma and translates in the blend's wealth of positive features. When the bouquet opens with notes of flowers and fresh fruit, followed by dried fruit, developing along complex toasted notes and ending with a harmony of spices, it means that the mixture has depth;

- potency: this character refers to the blend's body and to its aromatic robustness intended primarily as intensity and persistence of the aroma. Potency may take on a negative value when there is a lack of perfection: in short, a coffee blend can be very potent even when it is characterized by strong unpleasant scent, astringency and woodiness.

AXIOMS AND POSTULATES IN THE CREATION OF A BLEND

The creation of a blend is basically a work of art based on professional maturity, skill, knowledge, sensibility and passion.

This means there is no set of rules, no recipe one can follow to make an excellent blend. There are however some useful principles one can follow to avoid major mistakes:

- a good blend is based on affinities and complementarity, never on contrasts;

- blend creation follows the rule of multiplication: therefore one negative component does not simply coexist with the positive ones, but makes the entire result negative;

- small quantities of killer molecules can depress the depth of the whole blend.

HOW MANY COMPONENTS FOR A HIGH QUALITY BLEND?

The term "blend" takes on very different meanings depending on where it is pronounced: in many countries, a blend is simply the combination of two different coffees (different species, different origins or different processes after the harvest). In Italy, a blend is a form of art that emanates from a precise philosophy of the coffee company.

One of the most common questions is precisely how many components should a blend be made of in order to deliver an excellent cup of coffee. Two components are certainly not many, but many components do not necessarily lead to excellence.

There is no fixed recipe, but we can consider a set of three different alternatives:

- complexity is achieved through the combination of several coffee typologies (9–13);

- complexity is achieved through the combination of few types of coffee that are roasted in different ways;

- complexity is achieved with few typologies of perfectly roasted high-quality coffees

ROASTING SINGLE-ORIGIN COFFEES OR BLENDS

Different origin coffees can be roasted separately and then mixed together according to a set ratio or, alternatively, beans can be mixed when still green and then be roasted. These are two different methods, both used around the world, each requiring a specific workflow and the adoption of appropriate equipment. Once the choice is made it is difficult to reverse it. The roasting of single origins is certainly a way to enhance the qualities of the product. This method also allows making minor corrections in the mixture ratio in order to achieve a better result. On the other hand, this method is more costly, and there are some coffee producers who affirm that the roasting of all the different beans together delivers a better aromatic bouquet.

There is always the third way: mixing a part of the components before roasting and completing the blend afterwards.

ROASTING

COFFEE GRINDING

FROM MORTARS TO ELECTRONIC
DOSER GRINDERS

The coffee bean is a treasure chest. Although roasting has made the Coffea seed less elastic, its aroma and active molecules are well sealed inside scarcely permeable cells. As a consequence, in order to prepare a good cup of coffee the beans must be finely crushed so that water, in most cases very hot if not boiling, can penetrate into the coffee extracting the delicious beverage. By reducing the size of the bean, the contact surface between water and coffee is increased and the distance that the solvent must cover to penetrate the coffee cells is radically reduced. This is made possible by roasting: heat makes the beans hard, giving them an almost glassy and therefore friable consistence, making the roasted beans somewhat similar to coal, also under the rheological profile.

Once the mortar was the only tool available. Either in stone (preferably) or metal it was composed of two pieces (mortar and pestle). Grinding coffee beans in a mortar is certainly hard work, but the coffee is not heated, therefore the aromatic loss is very limited.

Obviously the level of fragmentation depends on the level of roasting, and on the strength and the number of hits of the pestle inside the crater.

In the search for something less rudimentary, humanity resorted to grinders as those used for spices, that is cylinders equipped with mechanisms capable of powdering pepper grains, a spice that was famed as a panacea for many ills and as a powerful aphrodisiac.

But coffee was different: not only are its beans much larger than pepper grains, but the quantities needed for the preparation of the beverage are much greater.

Therefore a different tool was needed, a faster instrument equipped with a more capacious container. The solution was found in the construction of a rotating mill mounted onto a shaft attached to the bean container driven by a crank of suitable length, that could capture and fragment the beans, forcing them into the narrow space created by the movement of the grinder. The old grinders were not very different from those still used today. The main difference was they were manual. Coffee grinding was usually a task entrusted to children and servants.

These machines first appeared rather late, during the seventeenth century, and were greeted with great favor becoming a household status symbol: those who owned one drank the exclusive coffee beverage.

The first patented model was registered in 1798 in the US by Thomas Bruff. After that came the coffee grinder designed by British smith Richard Dearman in 1799 and the 1815 model by another Briton, Achibald Kenrick, who equipped the tool with a regulation screw that could vary the fineness of the grind, an innovation that was to prove fundamental since it adapted the powder to the needs of the different preparation methods.

In 1818, the American Increase Wilson invented the support for fitting the grinder onto the wall making it much more comfortable to use in case of large scale production, while his compatriot Charles Parker built robust grinders for domestic use. Coffee consumption at that stage was on the rise, and nobody wanted to go without it even while travelling, so small travel grinders with a folding crank were invented. The tool however entered the world of industry in 1842 with the partnership between the French Peugeot brothers and the British Jackson brothers.

Industrialized coffee grinding arrived in Italy only in the late nineteenth century with the birth of the Tre Spade of the Bortolo brothers. But then, the advent of espresso coffee, which is the preparation that is the most sensitive to the grain size of the grind, led to the growth of world-class brands.

Obviously, the introduction of electric motors made the grinding process easier and faster. In the industrialized and professional sphere, the mechanism remains basically the same, but the grinders are perfected in terms of construction materials, geometry and precision. The introduction of electronics allowed the invention of grinding machines that can instantly grind the amount of powder needed for a cup of coffee also establishing a communication between the coffee-making machine and the grinder-dispenser regulating its action.

Electric motors were also applied to coffee grinders, creating electric blade grinders, a terrible invention that heats the coffee dispersing its aroma while producing very uneven powder limiting the coffee machine performance.

FROM MORTARS TO ELECTRONIC DOSER GRINDERS

Modern doser grinders were first invented in the 1920s. Before that, coffee was ground manually in the back of the shop, usually once a day. It was hard work.

The key feature of this tool is the possibility to adjust the grind size by regulating the distance between upper and lower burr: kept close, the burrs will produce a fine grind, kept further apart the result will be a coarser grind. All coffees are different, therefore there is no universal grinding rule but there are some grinds that better suit specific coffee qualities. But there is more: the ideal grind size of a batch of coffee beans can also depend on its moisture content and its age.

Available on the market there are flat and conical burr grinders. The choice essentially depends on the amount of grinding that will have to be carried out in a unit of time. Flat burr grinders, as we will explain later, are more suitable for intense work volumes throughout the day.

Conical burr grinders on the contrary can handle a heavy flow of work, especially at peak times when the grinder works virtually non-stop. Both types can be fitted with a doser or work "on demand," that is supplying 0.2 to 0.5 ounces (7–15 grams) of coffee directly to the filter of the coffee machine when needed. This kind of equipment is becoming increasingly popular since it avoids oxidation of powdered coffee that occurs when the coffee powder remains in the doser for some time. These models are also easier to clean.

THE LONG JOURNEY TO ESPRESSO COFFEE

Although we are restricting our study to the two main coffee species (Arabica and Canephora), coffee could be described, not unlike humanity, as an immense population of individuals all different from each other by virtue of their genes, combined with climate conditions, soil and even sun exposure of each single drupe. As if this were not enough, the coffee fruits can be processed in many different ways and coffee beans are affected by storage conditions and level of roasting. Last but not least, the preparation methods are decisive in defining the sensorial properties of the coffee we will taste in our cup.

Over the centuries, all these factors have varied continuously, by virtue of climatic, economic and social change, and also due to the introduction of new inventions and innovations.

Let's take a look at the journey coffee has undertaken throughout history, trying to imagine what might have been the sensorial profiles of the different coffees that were brewed along the way.

DRUPE DECOCTION

A decoction of coffee drupes was certainly the first and oldest way of making a coffee beverage, delivering a drink that retained the plant's healthy qualities, making water salutary (to a certain extent) while providing a good quantity of organic acids, minerals, and even carbohydrates.

A coffee drupe decoction is certainly nothing like the coffee we know today: on the one hand because it has no trace of the aromatic bouquet that develops with roasting and on the other because a cup of coffee decoction will always be more markedly bitter and astringent than sweet, although we may posit that those who used to drink it only picked ripe drupes (that is with about 23-25% sugar in them). Ultimately this method was lengthy and delivered a rather unpleasant drink.

Coffee decoctions are still made today, but using only the skin of desiccated and lightly roasted drupes. Some like it, but it is nothing like the coffee we enjoy today.

A tinplate coffee pot with a wooden handle of the kind used in the eighteenth and nineteenth centuries. This kind of early and rudimental pot brewed coffee by infusing it in boiling water.

WAYS OF MAKING COFFEE

SEED DECOCTION

Early-nineteenth-century Parisian magistrate and food enthusiast Brillat Savarin pre-scribed that coffee must come to a boil three times. This is a time-honored method of coffee making commonly known as Turkish coffee, a method that UNESCO has included in the world's intangible heritage list.

Certainly this method makes the most of coffee that in this case should be ground rather coarsely in order to make the drink clearer.

This method is certainly not a fast one, and from a sensory standpoint it does have some flaws: first of all, some coffee powder can get into your mouth while drinking it; and additionally some of the most elegant aromas are lost in the process and the scent of "cooked" coffee can emerge rather vigorously.

In this Cezve-like copper pot, coffee was extracted by infusing it in boiling water.

This type of coffee pot known as Dellal was used for five centuries in all regions of Arabia, Syria and Mesopotamia.

PERCOLATED COFFEE

The prospect of having a cup of coffee without any unpleasant coffee powder getting into your mouth inspired many to try and find a solution: a French textbook of 1832, for instance, explains how to use gelatin to clarify coffee. A method that the author himself admitted caused the loss of most of the coffee's finest aroma.

To achieve this goal, the simplest way was to pour hot water onto the coffee powder that was to be placed into a filter chamber retaining it. This idea was a good one, and percolation is today's most common coffee-making method, although carried out with different variants and equipment.

Obviously the extraction of the coffee beverage is directly related to the bean's level of grinding. The finer the coffee the longer the preparation. This means that a lot of coffee must be prepared at the same time, in order to have it ready when necessary. This causes a loss of sensorial quality, since heated coffee – or coffee kept at a certain temperature for a long time – loses much of its flavor and properties.

In order to avoid this, nineteenth century inventors worked hard to find a way of making percolation faster. Many solutions were found and some of them were patented. Let's take a look at the main ones.

Compared to regular percolation coffee pots, this 1854 invention patented by Griffiths & Co. of Birmingham assured higher water pressure during the extraction process.

With this type of 1850–1860 coffee pot you could brew coffee with the vacuum, press, percolation or filter system.

This exquisite French coffee pot (1820-1830) worked with a filter system. This innovation was an important evolution in the history of coffee preparation, separating the beverage from the ground beans.

This 1950s French coffee pot brewed coffee by percolation. The chamber above the filter was removed after the coffee was brewed and the porcelain pot was sealed with its coordinate lid.

The base of this coffee pot is in aluminum, while the removable upper part could complement an elegant table spread. This 1960–1970 coffee machine extracted the beverage through steam pressure.

This French coffee pot designed by Bouillon & Siry patented in 1872 was very popular in France and in Britain. The water was pumped to the surface and repeatedly filtered through the ground coffee.

GRAVITY

The traditional shape of a basic coffee percolator is that of an inverted cone. Obviously the coffee powder placed inside the cone will have different levels of thickness, thus offering varying levels of resistance to the passing of the water, determining diverse levels of coffee extraction.

In finding its way through the coffee powder, water also generates landslides and agglomerations creating pathways while being drawn down by gravity. Therefore, inventors focused on finding ways of improving this aspect in order to assure an even layer of coffee powder and a uniform spreading of the hot water that will pass through it. That was how the first filter coffee maker came about, and the man responsible for its invention was the Archbishop of Paris Jean-Baptiste de Belloy, no less.

In 1802, however, Henrion patented a double-chamber coffee maker to keep coffee warm, a concept that was later abandoned by Hadrot (1806), who however perfected the stability of the panel by introducing a press able to regulate the compactness of the coffee layer and assure an even distribution of water. In terms of the beverage's sensorial properties, Hadrot also tried to address the problem of iron: at the time coffee pots were made of iron, a metal that interacts with the phenolic acids of coffee releasing a metallic taste. Hadrot invented a coffee pot with a tin and bismuth alloy filter.

*Early twentieth-century tinplate
Neapolitan flip coffee pot.*

Early twentieth-century French flip nickel-plated brass coffee pot. Known as "Russian egg," this coffee pot came with a structure that allowed the rotation necessary to brew the beverage.

With Hadrot the concept of producing coffee machines with a metallic filter became somewhat established. An interesting innovation was introduced by tinsmith Morize (1819), who patented a coffee pot that had to be turned upside-down, combining the container for heating the water and the one for the collection of coffee: the ancestor of the Neapolitan flip coffee pot.

Optimization of the panel and of water diffusion had made the coffee-making process slightly faster, but what people wanted was strong coffee, possibly without using a lot of coffee. To this end, the key factors became temperature, grind size, and time of interaction between water (the solvent) and coffee powder.

If you remove boiling water from the fire and place it against a cold surface (the coffee layer it

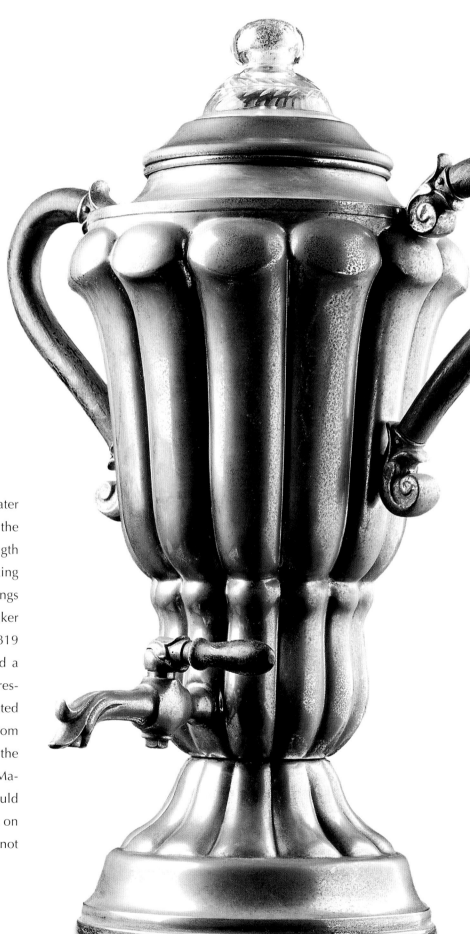

must go through), the temperature of that water will drop, a circumstance that does not affect the speed of the preparation, but rather the strength of the beverage. And while for us today working at lower temperatures is considered a plus, things were different in those days. The flip coffee maker limited the problem of water cooling, but in 1819 a man named Laurens invented and patented a pump circulation coffee machine with a pressure-tight lower chamber where water, heated by a lamp, was pushed into a manifold and from there distributed onto the coffee located in the upper chamber. A further step was taken by Madame Jeanne Richard's 1837 coffee pot that could regulate the intensity of coffee by recycling it on the panel. The outcome was a very strong but not very fine tasting coffee.

VACUUM COFFEE POTS

In the first half of the nineteenth century, coffee-making techniques incorporated the use of vacuum in hermetically closed two-chamber systems. One chamber contained water and was to be placed over a source of heat and the other contained the coffee powder. When the water reached the right temperature, the pot was removed from the heat source, causing the water to cool down thereby creating a depression that sucked the liquid up into the second chamber that contained the coffee. Dozens of vacuum coffee machine patents were registered, becoming a rather popular method especially when they could be safely produced in solid glass. Only rarely were these models made of metal. This method made percolation faster, but these coffee pots were fragile and rather tricky to use and also to clean, ultimately making the entire process rather time consuming. On the other hand, coffee made with these vacuum pots was excellent from a sensorial standpoint. The process is also quite spectacular to look at and this kind of coffee pot is quite common in Asia where many cafes have them, nowadays in ameliorated versions easier to use.

This vacuum coffee machine was patented in 1855 in Vienna. Its "scales" structure made the entire coffee making process mechanical.

HYDRAULIC PRESSURE

The first hydraulic pressure coffee-pots were invented in 1830 by the Frenchman Count Réal and then in 1854 by the Englishman Loysel. With their inventions coffee was brewed by creating a column of water placed above the ground coffee, a process that led to the commendable result of being able to use a much finer grind and therefore increasing the effectiveness of the coffee extraction process. Of the two, Loysel's coffee pot became particularly popular: refined and monumental models of it were produced throughout the nineteenth century and beyond.

Late nineteenth-century British silver plate Napierian coffee maker.

VAPOR PRESSURE

The power of steam has been known since the time of the ancient Greeks, but the nineteenth century was the century of steam par excellence, with the invention of the steam engine for instance, an innovation that aptly replaced animal workforce in many ambits. The world of coffee-making was not immune to this avenue of progress either, and inventors immediately incorporated steam to the coffee brewing process – a procedure that apart from a few exceptions always requires heat and water. One of the first patents we know of dates to 1932 and was presented by Louis Bernard Rabaud who invented a coffee pot where water was pushed through the panel by means of vapor pressure: basically a forerunner of the Italian moka pot. Rabaud's invention was followed by Samuel Parker's fountain coffee machine (1833), Alexandre Lebrun's coffee pot (1838), by Giovanni Maria Loggia's in 1857, in 1878 by Eike's double chamber coffee pot, and by other larger coffee machines, such as those invented by Angelo Moriondo in 1884 and Luigi Bezzera in 1905.

These results opened the door to espresso coffee as we know it today: even though these machines hardly reached two atm, they were faster and assured a better extraction. But their effectiveness was dependent on high temperature, a factor that tends to spoil the aroma contained in plant cells.

Produced between 1920 and 1930 by La Lombarda, this electric coffee maker brewed coffee using steam pressure.

103 top This Italian 1960s electric coffee maker could simultaneously pour four coffees out of its spouts.

103 bottom This mid twentieth-century coffee maker with incorporated alarm was produced by Gaude, Turin: at a set time an electric resistance would activate, pouring the coffee into the cup, and in turn the cup with its weight would set off the alarm.

This Italian Belle Époque coffee machine could brew either two or four cups of coffee at a time.

This 1905 coffee machine, one of the first designed for bars, is characterized by its vertical shape and by the gas burner to create pressure in the chamber.

A 1920-1930 domestic espresso coffee machine whose design is very similar to that of larger professional machines that were used in bars.

MECHANICAL PRESSURE

Steam is an excellent resource, but not the optimal one for coffee. Francesco Illy understood this back in 1935 when he patented a compressed air machine. Achille Gaggia in 1947 patented a coffee machine with a spring mechanism capable of exerting a pressure of about eight atmospheres on the water.

This invention, combined with the progress achieved by hundreds of coffee roasters over one century, eventually led to the creation of the Italian Espresso coffee. The final step was taken by Faema that in 1960 invented a machine that applied pressure by means of a volumetric pump: the following year the historic Faema E61 was launched on the market.

This 1950s coffee machine worked by manual pressure. The water had to be heated separately and then pushed through the ground coffee by lowering the two levers.

WHAT ARE THE DIFFERENCES?

When talking about coffee, these terms are sometimes used as synonyms although they are not. They correspond to very different extraction techniques. Let's take a look:

- percolation: extraction is achieved by making a fluid pass through a porous substance;

- decoction: an extraction method based on boiling;

- infusion: the ingredient is soaked in hot water to extract its soluble elements.

- maceration: extraction technique carried out at room temperature or in a cooled environment (crio-maceration) creating contact between a liquid and a the ingredient.

In coffee-making these systems can coexist (infusion and percolation, for instance) but if we were to indicate the prevalent technique for every method we would have to say that Turkish coffee is a decoction, coffee made with piston pots is an infusion, and cold brews are the result of maceration, and all other methods are forms of percolation.

The piston pressure coffee machines became common in bars and at home, marking the beginning of the coffee-cream era.

WATER AND COFFEE

To what extent do the characteristics of water affect a cup of coffee's sensorial properties? What innovative means can be used to keep a coffee machine in good working order without diminishing the quality of the blend?

The importance attributed to water in the preparation of beverages is to some extent legendary and water is often attributed the general responsibility of the sensorial characteristics of the drink as a whole, almost as if water were to determine a sort of indication of geographical origin. Clear examples of this can be found in the beer and whisky making industry. Over a century ago the Japanese believed so firmly in this principle that they tried to reproduce a water in their country that shared the same characteristics of Scottish water in order to start a production of whisky. An endeavor that eventually turned out to be very successful.

Coffee was no exception. Entire populations attributed to water the merit of the quality of their famed espresso coffee: Naples is a clear example of this.

Water, the universal coffee solvent, clearly has its importance, so let's try to understand more about the mechanisms that rule the water/coffee relation in the making of espresso coffee.

THE CHARACTERISTICS OF WATER AND ITS INTERACTION WITH COFFEE
Basically there are three aspects of water that have an impact on the preparation of espresso coffee.

- presence of chlorine: water chlorination is a public health measure, but it is certainly something that does not do improve the quality of our cup of coffee. Although the amount of chlorine dissolved in drinking water has gradually reduced over the years, this element has nonetheless a strong oxidizing power. An effect that is increased by heat, acting on the fats and influencing the formation of the cream;

- presence of anomalous smells: anomalous smells in water can be due to different substances. Among the worst of these are sulfur compounds that directly affect the sensorial properties of coffee, covering the floral and fresh fruity notes;

- presence of calcium salts and magnesium, which increase the hardness of water.

The negative effect produced by chlorine is that it reduces the cream in espresso coffee and covers a whole range of very pleasing aromas, in particular the floral notes that are highly favored by most coffee lovers.

The anomalous smells are less subtle. In general, their presence should serve as a warning not to use that particular type of water, but on a sensory level their effect may vary. They might reduce the aromatic intensity, cancel a whole series of aromatic nuances, or even bring out anomalous scents that would not be otherwise perceptible.

Chlorine and anomalous smells can be avoided in two ways: using water that is chlorine and odor free or pitchers and activated carbon filters that can eliminate them.

But let's focus on the third point: hardness in water is due to a combination of anions (sulphates, carbonates, etc.) and cations (calcium, magnesium and others). The elements of this combination divide into two groups: permanent and temporary hardness, that together determine the overall hardness of the water, the parameter that normally appears on the common kits on the market.

Permanent hardness is mainly due to the presence of calcium sulfate, which is not removed by heating the water, while temporary hardness is due to carbonates that with heat can produce incrustations on the coffee machine equipment.

And here we get to the critical point: hard water makes better coffee, but this quality is in conflict with the need to keep espresso machines clean and efficient. Calcium is a key factor to obtain body, syrupiness, and a stable and elastic cream. This cation in fact improves the formation of a network of proteins that as the coffee pours into the cup incorporates carbohydrate colloids and due to the action of the residual carbon dioxide contained in coffee and to the diversity of weight density, rises to the surface creating the cream.

Normally the process to make water softer is carried out by replacing calcium with sodium, another cation that has a different behavior. Especially if the pH is reduced (rise in acidity), not only does sodium have a certain aggressiveness towards metals, but it also tends to make thin coffee, with little and scarcely elastic cream. To improve espresso making while assuring a proper working of the coffee machine, innovative professional and domestic methods have been developed: filters that combine limescale protection with elimination of unwanted substances.

COFFEE MAKING METHODS

As we have seen, people have always liked coffee and therefore, over the centuries, humanity has worked towards finding ways of making the best brew, inventing different methods based on their level of knowledge, different possibilities and beliefs, defining a wide series of techniques each one with its different way of treating this product of nature, and each one delivering very different results. Except for decoction of the drupes, we cannot say that there is one single prevailing way of making coffee. Different cultures have different methods.

ESPRESSO COFFEE

A cup of espresso coffee is obtained by forcing water through a layer of coffee, delivering a polyphasic beverage with a combination of soluble, suspended and emulsified compounds. In truth, all types of coffee share these same characteristics, but espresso coffee not only particularly highlights the suspended and emulsified compounds, but also stands out for the special relation it creates between the two and the soluble compounds.

Towards the end of the nineteenth century, coffee was a common beverage that had been a habit in the western countries for at least three centuries. Over that period of time, many systems for its preparation had been developed. The task however was not a simple one, because it wasn't only about making a coffee infusion: the process had to be fast so that the coffee could be drunk freshly brewed, while still retaining all the goodness it extracted from the powder, leaving the least noble components in the exhausted ground coffee.

Basically the world of coffee worked hard for at least three centuries to satisfy three strongly interconnected necessities:

- rapidity: if it is true that coffee is especially appreciated for its caffeine, the quickest way to take it from the plant would be to eat a coffee leaf salad or a few cherries, raw or boiled, as they did in the olden days. Today with globalization there would certainly be a way of making fresh deliveries of these products every day. But only "taste masochists" would enjoy this kind of products. We do not know who had the first stroke of genius, but the idea of roasting the seeds made all the difference, since only through heat do the coffee beans take on the exquisite aroma we all know and appreciate. Also exceptional is the fact that relatively small amounts of water can extract the coffee's fine constituents. Hot or cold water? Either, but cold water takes longer. So, although the cold extraction has been known since 1832, this technique is very slow and only rarely used. On the other hand, it is easy to see how brewing-speed increases with hot water. Therefore by increasing pressure, water surpasses its boiling temperature making the process faster and the beverage stronger. But by doing so, the resulting beverage is less pleasant in the mouth since a stronger extraction highlights bitterness and astringency, causing a loss of the most elegant aromas;

- strength: only very rarely do human senses fail in judging the physiological effect of food, and coffee is no exception. It is a fact that since its origins, strong coffee has always been perceived as a beverage that has great effect on the nervous system. The strength of coffee is determined by three factors: aroma intensity, consistency (body or syrupiness) and bitterness. Three are the variants that can determine the strength of a cup of coffee: species (Canephora beans – Robusta belongs to this species – make stronger coffee than Arabica), roasting, and extraction. Dark roast Robusta beans will give a stronger cup of coffee, but one with a less pleasant feel in the mouth.

It is a fact that in the early days of coffee in Europe (in the 1600s), Arabica was the only choice. But we are led to believe it must have been a rather poor choice if a French nobleman, a guest of the Ambassador of Sultan Mehmed, felt the need to take a little sugar from the bird bowl to add it to his cup of coffee. The flavor of the beverage was so much improved that from that moment onwards (1669) even the Ambassador started to use it.

Sugar not only psychologically compensates bitterness but also adds body while increasing aroma persistence. So much so that, as German anatomist and botanist Johann Vesling noted in 1638 while in Cairo, sugar was already used in Egypt where coffee drupes were even candied. Coffee however, was an expensive product, and people used to make the most of it. Not so much by roasting, which, given the means available at the time, was probably carried out rather approximatively, with more than a few burnt beans, but rather through extraction: coffee in fact was boiled over and over again, up to ten or twelve times. In the early days, in fact, coffee was made the Turkish way: water was brought to the boil in the classic double truncated-cone copper pot, then the coffee powder added to the water that was then put back onto the stove. When the water came to a boil again, the beverage was removed once more from the heat until it boiled down and then returned to the heat one last time. Brillat Savarin prescribed not to repeat the process more than three times, but not only was Savarin a refined gourmand: he was also a very rich man. The poor people used to boil the coffee over and over again only to smell the aroma of coffee.

- pleasure: when something makes us feel good, our brain classifies it as useful and that is why we like it even if there are adverse signals that would normally depress our level of pleasure. This is why we accept bitterness in beer, in certain liqueurs, and in coffee. However, when bitterness combines with astringency (that unpleasant sense of dryness in our mouth) that product becomes unacceptable. In the past, species was not a problem as it is today that Robusta is so widespread on the market, but approximate roasting that often caused beans to burn and the repeated boiling of the water and coffee certainly reduced the pleasure of the brew. If on the one hand the presence of coffee powder in the drink made the coffee stronger, on the other it was unpleasant when it reached the mouth and also increased the sense bitterness and the astringency. Ameliorations were made on the shape of the coffee pots to improve the brewing, and filters were introduced into the pouring spout, refining the cup quality of the beverage, but without solving the problem. People wanted their cup of coffee black and hot, freshly made and not heated, because another problem was that of the fat components turning rancid, a problem that may manifest itself in the beans only a few days after they are roasted (if they are not covered), in the coffee powder a few hours after grinding, and only a few minutes after brewing.

ESPRESSO FROM THE BAR

Certainly it was not only the need to make coffee quickly that determined the success of espresso coffee and of the millions of bars serving it all over the world: a cup of espresso, if prepared to perfection, remains an unsurpassed pleasure. Although the filter system still maintains its supremacy worldwide, it has been estimated that today there are more than two million professional coffee machines making espresso coffee. And by "professional machines" we mean those that are entrusted to the care of a bartender in charge of choosing the mixture that he personally grinds while knowingly operating the machine. So we are not talking about the super automatic espresso electronic machines that, although very smart and efficient, can't count on the human factor that makes the espresso coffee so much nicer.

The evolution of coffee machines however has significantly contributed to the evolution of espresso coffee itself and still today a good coffee machine can make a difference in terms of quality.

The espresso machine, the heart of the method, has Italian roots: at the 1857 Brescia exhibition, Giovanni Loggia presented a steam coffee machine and in 1884 Angelo Moriondo, patented a large coffee machine capable of satisfying the needs of a café. In 1901, this machine was perfected by Milanese engineer Luigi Bezzera, who in turn patented his own and improved coffee machine. Step after step, we get to 1970 when the first coffee machines with multiple boilers appeared. The aim of this technological innovation was that of reaching maximum stability combined with thermal flexibility in order to improve the final coffee brew. In these machines, steam production was separated from the heating of water used to brew the coffee. In the 1980s, the first super-automatic machines appeared with one or more incorporated doser grinders.

Today, technology is evermore present in the evolution of coffee machines. This has led to a high level of automation and high flexibility in terms of temperature regulation allowing coffee makers to customize the final product to the maximum. Today on the market, there are several systems to heat the water needed for a cup of espresso, namely the heat exchanger system, the lever system and the separate boiler system.

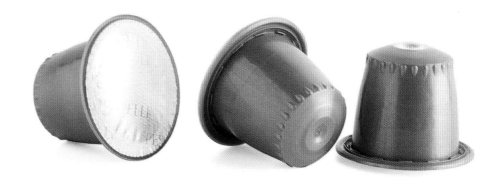

CERTIFIED ITALIAN ESPRESSO

A cup of Italian Espresso coffee is dark-brown and is topped with a tawny hazel-color cream. The cream is very fine, with a thick bubble-less texture. The aroma is intense with clear notes of flowers, fruit, toasted bread and chocolate, all sensations that can be perceived even after the coffee is swallowed, in the persistent aroma that can last for many seconds, sometimes even for minutes. The taste is round, consistent and velvety, acidity and bitterness are well balanced without one prevailing on the other and there is no or only very little astringency.

This is how the Italian National Espresso Institute (established in 1998) defines espresso coffee, to assure the consumer the greatest pleasure, also providing a chart of blends, doser grinders, machines, and baristas.

The espresso coffee that is served in bars is not a ready drink: it is prepared on the spot and therefore the barista who actually makes it is essential towards the creation of an impeccable cup of coffee. The barista chooses the blend, adjusts the doser grinder so that the grind is appropriate and regulates the pressure and temperature of the machine. Other decisive elements towards a good result are the barista's senses and some simple physical parameters: the barista must make 0.5 fl oz (25 ml) of coffee in 25 seconds with water at about 194 °F (90 °C) with a 9 bar pressure.

ESPRESSO AT HOME

The espresso that we can make ourselves at home today is a direct descent of the beverage we are served at the bar, although the same level of perfection has not been reached yet. The reason is simple: for commercial reasons domestic equipment must be much cheaper and much easier to use, and this is why its performance is not quite at the same level. Currently there are two systems to make espresso coffee at home: capsules and automatic machines.

CAPSULES

At the end of the last century, home espresso making was made simple by the invention of coffee pods: a single dose of ground and pressed coffee powder packed into a paper filter. That was a great invention because it made espresso at home quick and easy and not too different from that served at the bar. This idea also paved the way to the spread of new single-origin types of coffee that could be tasted on their own, thus giving coffee lovers the chance to try new flavors and increase their knowledge of coffee from distant countries. The next step was the invention of espresso coffee capsules: 0.1 to 0.2 oz (5–7 g) of coffee powder packed into small plastic or metal cases in different shapes and sizes that have to be inserted into a machine capable of supplying water under pressure for more or less 15 seconds.

Pods and capsules today represent a large share of the coffee market all over the world and are beginning to spread even to bars where due to volume of business or to other factors a professional espresso machine would not be a suitable option.

AUTOMATIC ESPRESSO MACHINES

These clever machines can instantly grind 0.1 to 0.3 oz (5–10 g) of coffee and make a cup of espresso in 15 to 20 seconds. Compared to coffee capsules, this system has a lower impact on the environment and, once the investment is recovered, it does lead to considerable savings. Moreover, this system allows consumers to explore single-origin coffees and experience new flavors.

OTHER TYPES OF ESPRESSO

Espresso coffee has now spread all over the world with millions of operating espresso machines. But not all espresso coffees are like the Italian espresso. To make an Italian espresso you use 0.2 oz (7 g) of coffee powder to make 0.5 fl oz (25 ml) of coffee in the cup. But in other countries, a cup of espresso is made with 0.3 oz (10 g) of coffee powder or more, and in some cultures an ideal cup of espresso can even be of 1.6 fl oz (50 ml).

But there is more: technically, even the coffee made by vending-machines (like those installed in workplaces and in many public places) is an espresso. In many cases, distorted commercial logics have caused a dramatic loss of quality in the making of espresso coffee, which in these cases is no grand flavorsome experience. This is essentially due to the poor quality of the coffee that is used in these vending machines, and to their incorrect cleaning and maintenance. Nowadays these machines are equipped with excellent extraction technology that could provide a very good coffee.

THE FILTER SYSTEM

The filter system is a coffee brewing technique based on gravity percolation of water preheated at about 203 °F (95 °C). About 0.3 to 0.5 oz (10–15 g) of coffee make an about 6.7 fl oz (200 ml) cup of coffee. The filter is the system for those who like to drink plenty of coffee: a brew with little body, but that if made properly, has little bitterness, balanced acidity, and good olfactory impact. This method is the most common around the world, much in use in countries where people are great coffee consumers, as in Northern Europe and the United States.

Historically, the filter method was the third process to be introduced in the world of coffee. If the drupes decoction did not provide a satisfactory result from a sensorial standpoint and was only some-

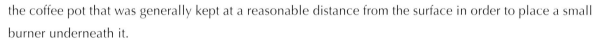

thing that the inhabitants of the cultivation areas enjoyed, the boiling of ground roasted coffee beans provided a beverage with residues that inevitably ended up in the mouth. So, that is why in the 1700s, people came up with a different method, and began to put the coffee in a cloth bag that was then immersed in boiling water. A man named Donmartin perfected this technique by hooking the bag to the upper part of the coffee pot that was generally kept at a reasonable distance from the surface in order to place a small burner underneath it.

Coffee was so important that even the archbishop of Paris Jean Baptiste Belloy (1709–1808) designed his own coffee pot, introducing a simple but very effective innovation: he divided the pot into two chambers – a lower cylindrical chamber, with a spout equipped with a stopper and handle, and the upper part, also cylindrical, equipped with a filter at the base and a lid at the top. With this system people could brew a coffee that was full of aroma. This technique was so successful that Belloy's coffee machine became the coffee maker par excellence and examples of it are still used today. Henrion and Hadrot perfected this invention in the early nineteenth century.

The filter system, based on gravity percolation, was the forefather of many other systems that followed, each with their own pros and cons, such as, for instance, the coffee powder placed into a canvas cone filter into which boiling hot water was poured, the double-chamber coffee maker with the coffee held up by a metal filter, the double filter system to obtain a more homogeneous layer of coffee, the immersion filter for great quantities (great yield but little quality), and so on. In the meantime, new water heating systems were also being developed, inventions that would eventually lead to electric machines capable of pouring hot water onto the coffee, as well as new types of filters.

Today, the simplicity of this method has significantly expanded the possibilities: from the single-dose kits used in Japan (and elsewhere) with cup, filter, coffee, sugar and powdered milk, ready to be used wherever one can find sufficiently hot water, to the large coffee machines capable of making great quantities of coffee for community meetings and conferences.

In the world of coffee lovers and of different coffee preparation and serving methods, we have seen the spread of filter systems based on skill and mastery that are also to some extent stage-effective and that have been adopted in cafes as ways to introduce new consumers to new coffee experiences. So let's take a look at the main filter systems, old and new.

NEAPOLITAN FLIP COFFEE POT

History is based on written records, and the invention of the Neapolitan flip coffee pot dates to 1819 and is attributed to a Frenchman named Morize. Yet nobody can say whether such a technique existed before or whether or not it was in use in Naples. In any case, this type of coffee pot became famous in Naples, perhaps due to this city's love for strong roasts that produce a coffee with great aroma even using a filter coffee maker. But the opposite could also be true: the love for strong-tasting coffee may have induced Neapolitans to roast the coffee beans more in order to maximize the flavor extraction of the flip coffee pot that, however slow, since it mostly relies on gravity, has less extraction power than a moka or espresso machine. Initially Neapolitan flip coffee pots were made in copper, and from 1886 in aluminum. Nowadays, the stainless steel versions are the most common.

Also known as *cuccumella*, this coffee pot is generally cylindrical and consists of one chamber for water, one chamber for the brewed coffee, and a central section for the coffee powder composed of a double filter to allow the passage of water through the coffee powder layer.

To prepare a cup of coffee with a Neapolitan flip coffee pot, you start by filling the water chamber that features a small hole that prevents the creation of internal pressure and signals when the water has come to the boil. Then you put some coarsely ground coffee in the filter that must then be closed and placed into its specific compartment. Then the container for the collection of the brewed coffee must be put in place and the coffee pot is ready to go on the heat. When the water comes to a boil, the coffee pot must be turned upside down so that gravity will draw the hot water through the coffee layer, delivering the brewed coffee in what now has become the lower chamber. The process takes between 5 to 10 minutes, mostly depending on the grain size of the coffee powder.

CHEMEX

A direct descendent of the Erlenmeyer flask used in chemistry, the Chemex coffeemaker was invented in 1941 in Germany by Dr Peter Schlumbohm. The Chemex is a single glass recipient in the shape of two truncated cones: the larger one at the bottom, where the brewed coffee is collected, the smaller and open one on top, where the filter is positioned.

Chemex coffeemakers come in different sizes, and can serve from three to six cups of coffee. The ideal ratio would require 0.5 oz (15 g) of coffee for each cup. So here is the process to make four 6.7 fl oz (200 ml) cups of coffee: take one liter of hot (203 °F/95 °C) water and place the paper filter in the upper cone of the pot. Rinse the filter well with some of the hot water, letting it run through the paper and then throw that water away.

Place the coffee in the filter and pour part of the hot water over it with a spiraling movement until the coffee powder is completely soaked. Wait for 45 seconds, and then pour another quarter of the water and wait again. You can also mix the wet powder with a wooden spoon, but every time you pour water you must wait 30 seconds before pouring some more. Once you have 28 fl oz (800 ml) of brewed coffee in the lower cone, the beverage is ready to be served.

Chemex paper filters are thicker than those used for other filter methods, and this makes the process slower contributing to a greater extraction. Chemex coffeepots also work with metallic filters that must be washed and thoroughly dried after use.

V60

The V60 coffee maker takes its name from its V-shaped 60° angle upper part where you place the filter, below which is the section collecting the brewed coffee.

Heat 21 fl oz (300 ml) of water to 203 °F (95 °C). Place the paper filter in the upper section and rinse it with about 3.5 fl oz (100 ml) of hot water in order to eliminate any papery flavor that you don't want to taste in your brew, wait for it to run into the lower section and then throw it away. Then place about 0.4 oz (13 g) of fairly coarse ground coffee. With controlled circular movements pour about 0.8 fl oz (25 ml) of hot water on top of the coffee powder and wait 30 seconds. Then add other 0.8 fl oz (25 ml) and wait another 15 seconds and so on until you have 7 fl oz (200 ml) of brewed coffee in the lower section. If the coffee grinding was correct, the extraction process should last between 2 and a half and 3 minutes. If it takes longer, it means the coffee beans were ground too finely. If it takes less, it means the powder was too coarse.

INFUSION, DECOCTION AND MACERATION

The love of coffee has led to countless experimentations, applying practically all the classical techniques that have been discovered over the centuries to extract all that is good and healthy from this product of nature. Some of these methods have become very popular, others less, but coffee lovers have never stopped experimenting and it does not look like they will be stopping anytime soon. So we must expect new techniques in the future, but meanwhile, let's take a look at the main preparation methods associated with the above mentioned techniques.

FRENCH PRESS

The French press is a piston coffee pot composed of a glass body set into a metal frame standing on four feet elevating the vessel from the surface and a piston with a filter edged by a spring whose function is to prevent grounds to bypass the filter and seep into the brew.

The mechanism is straightforward: you heat the glass body with some hot water, then add 0.4 oz (14 g) of coffee inside the glass jar and pour 7 fl oz

(200 ml) of 203 °F (95 °C) hot water making sure that the coffee powder is evenly soaked. Infuse for 4 minutes, then remove the foam that has formed on top, mount the piston and press it downwards compacting the coffee powder at the bottom of the pot. The coffee is ready to be served: depending on the fineness of the coffee powder and the time of infusion, the brew will have more or less body and aroma, and depending on the skill of the coffee maker and on the quality of the actual French press, the coffee will be more or less clear.

CLEVER COFFEE DRIPPER

This method originated in Taiwan, and requires a glass cone that fits on top of a vessel or mug that will contain the brewed coffee.

Heat water to 194–198 °F (90–92 °C) and use some of it to rinse the paper filter well after having placed it in the cone. Then put 0.4 oz (14 g) of ground coffee into the cone and pour 7 fl oz (200 ml) of hot water over it. Let the coffee brew for two and a half minutes and then let it filter. The operation should last about a minute.

AEROPRESS

This is one of the latest coffee-infusion methods. It was invented in 2005 by Alan Adler and consists of a cylinder ending with a filter with a piston moving inside it.

The mechanism is rather simple: heat some water to about 194–200 °F (90–93 °C). Use part of it to rinse the filter that must be then attached to the cylinder. Then insert 0.4 oz (14 g) of suitably ground

coffee and pour in 7 fl oz (200 ml) of water, making sure that the powder soaks homogeneously. Let the coffee infuse for 1 minute and then push the coffee through the filter with the piston, collecting the brewed coffee directly into the cup. This method can be personalized and the sensorial profile of the coffee can be adjusted to taste.

SYPHON

Invented in the first half of the nineteenth century, this coffee making method is certainly one of the most spectacular. A syphon coffee maker consists of a structure composed of two chambers – typically two glass spherical vessels – placed one on top of the other and connected in the middle by a filter.

To prepare a cup of coffee place 10.5 fl oz (300 ml) of water in the lower chamber that is connected to the top one where you will put 0.5 oz (15 g) of ground coffee. Then light the flame underneath the lower chamber and bring the water to a boil. Due to pressure, the water will rise up into the upper chamber where it will soak the coffee. Once all the water has reached the upper chamber, turn the heat off. This will cause a depression in the lower chamber sucking the coffee from the upper chamber down into the lower one through the filter. The coffee is then ready to be served.

To make the process faster (about 90 seconds) you can use pre-heated water.

COLD BREW

A 1832 manual mentions the cold-extraction coffee technique highlighting how this method completely modified the sensorial properties of the beverage by reducing the amount of bitter and astringent components and greatly preserving the aroma. The reason why this method did not spread is that it takes a long time: to make one liter of coffee you need from 6 to 24 hours, depending on taste. This method has many variants and several recipes have been proposed on the occasion of its bicentenary.

Essentially the cold brew equipment – also called cold drip, although the purists underline there are differences between the two – consists of a water chamber (or water and ice or only-ice chamber) placed above a filter containing coffee powder. Below is a container for the brewed coffee. The first step is to load the filter with rather coarse ground coffee and saturate it with water. Then place the collecting vessel underneath and regulate the tap that will pour out the brewed coffee at a rate of 6–10 drops every 10 seconds (about 0.1 fl oz/3 ml per minute). The coffee/water ratio should be of about 2.4 to 3.1 oz (70–90 g) every 35 fl oz/1 liter, so 0.2 to 0.3 oz (7–9 g) every 3.5 fl oz/100 ml.

WAYS OF MAKING COFFEE

GOTA A GOTA

This is a typical Peruvian method, for which you need a cylindrical coffee maker composed of two chambers of almost equal capacity. The top chamber is filled with coffee onto which, with a technique that requires experience, boiling water is poured gradually and many times, until the lower chamber is filled with essence. Yes, because in this case the brew is a real coffee essence, a syrup able to remain unaltered up to 72 hours and that can be diluted with hot water to taste. The process is very lengthy because the hot water must be added at regular intervals, whenever the powder starts to dry, and only in very little quantities with only very little liquid surfacing from the coffee powder.

The result is a very interesting brew from a sensorial standpoint, provided that the coffee powder is of high quality, duly roasted and ground.

TURKISH COFFEE

This is the second oldest coffee making method coming immediately after the drupe decoction on the coffee method timeline. Technically, Turkish coffee is a decoction, since it is obtained by boiling coffee powder in some water. We identify this method as Turkish coffee, since this is how UNESCO defined it in the world list of intangible heritage, but this technique is actually used in many other parts of the world, albeit with variants that developed over the course of its secular history, namely in many countries of the Middle East and throughout the Balkan peninsula and of course in Turkey.

Turkish coffee is prepared in a special copper or brass long-handled jug called ibrik or cezve that can be heated in hot sand or, as more common nowadays, over another source of heat. Pour 1.7 fl oz (50 ml) of water for every cup into the jug and bring it to a boil, then add a teaspoon of coffee and return to a boil. By removing the cezve from the heat source, the boiling stops and the foam that forms on the top can be removed. Bring back to a boil once more and then serve. Wait a few minutes for the coffee to settle at the bottom of the cup before drinking.

MOKA POT

The moka system is a steam-pressure method in the sense that it is the steam produced by the boiling water in the lower chamber that pushes the water through the coffee powder layer. In fact the moka pot is the descendent of the ingenious inventions of manufacturers such as Louis Bernard Rabaud (French), Romershausen (German), Samuel Parker (English), Lebrun (French), Angelo Loggia (Italian), and Eike (German). The moka pot as we know it today was invented by Bialetti in 1933.

Prior to Bialetti's patent, coffee in Italy was mostly brewed with percolation coffee machines, the Neapolitan flip coffee pot being the most common. But the moka, at first erroneously known as "the Milanese" coffee pot soon spread taking center stage. We will soon talk about the substantial differences between the two, but first we must clarify something: the moka coffee pot was born in Piedmont, in Omegna a town famous for its many skilled metalworkers. In the Neapolitan flip coffee pot it is simply gravity that draws hot water into the lower collection chamber through the coffee powder. So not only is the process slow and the slightest mistake in the grind – or the alteration in the coffee powder caused by humidity – may cause the procedure to become unnervingly long (and when you want a coffee, you can't wait forever), but also once the pot is removed from the flame to be turned upside down, the boiling water in the upper chamber gradually cools down becoming less effective in terms of extraction.

In the moka pot the reverse happens: the water is heated and pressure rises due to the water's effort to get through the coffee layer. This causes a much better extraction, delivering a coffee with better aroma and greater body.

Practical, lightweight, inexpensive, fast enough to keep up with the pace of modern times, and effective enough to extract more than other systems the best of what coffee beans have to offer: that's why the moka pot has enjoyed a level of success which is not easy to measure, but that is definitely huge. We could start by saying that every year about 15 million moka pots are sold worldwide.

If we consider that on average a moka pot lasts for about ten years, we could say that there are 150 million functioning moka pots in the world, at least one in every ten households on planet Earth. But because not everyone in the world drinks moka coffee, the percentage would rise well over 10% if we wanted to consider only those cultures that drink this beverage (for example in Italy, where the spread is equal to 90% of families, with at least 2 different-size mokas in each household).

Of the 15 million moka pots produced every year, 10 million are sold in Italy, which is the leading country in the sector, with its about 25 producers and 30 active company brands. In the rest of the world there are just about 15 other producers based in Spain (about 5 producers), Latin America, Germany and in a few other countries.

THE MOKA POT: COMPONENTS AND TECHNIQUE

Basically the moka is a coffee pot composed of a lower chamber where the water is heated, a central funnel-shaped filter that contains the coffee powder and which sinks into the water chamber stopping only a few millimeters from its base, and finally a jug-shape top section to collect the coffee with at the center a collector through which the extracted coffee flows upwards.

The physical principle the moka coffee method is based on is water's change of status from liquid to steam. In absence of heat, there is balance between the air and liquid inside the lower chamber under the filter. But when the temperature rises, pressure builds up and water can only find its way out through the terminal part of the coffee funnel-filter. When the built-up pressure is enough to contrast atmospheric pressure and the resistance of the coffee powder layer, the liquid flows up into the upper chamber where the brewed coffee is collected.

When all the water has made its way up to the upper section, steam can also come out producing the classic puff of steam telling us it is time to turn off the heat.

A good moka complies with these parameters:

- maximum water temperature during the extraction: 209 °F (98 °C);

- maximum pressure inside the lower chamber 2.5 bar;

- maximum temperature of the extracted coffee: 185 °F (85 °C);

- maximum quantity of coffee produced with every dose of coffee powder: 1.6 fl oz (50 ml);

- quantity of water left in the water chamber after the extraction: about 0.1 fl oz (5 ml) for each cup.

HOW TO CHOOSE THE PERFECT MOKA POT

Stainless steel or aluminum? This would seem to be the only decision to make when choosing a moka pot. But actually there are many other important factors to consider, many of which have an impact on the brewed coffee sensorial properties and on the length of the coffee pot's life.

Let's take a look:

- material: compared to aluminum, stainless steel certainly looks nicer, easier to clean and more resistant. But actually in more than one sensory test, aluminum has turned out to be superior to steel. Of course there are different qualities of aluminum and this must be considered too, but there are other details to consider:

- finterior finish, of the lower chamber especially: the smoother the better, since smooth surfaces are easier to keep clean. Asperities, abrasions, depressions and imperfections can affect the duration of the object and, gradually, the sensorial quality of the coffee;

- gasket: it is practically the only element of a moka pot that is subject to wear, especially if you screw the coffee pot tight with coffee grains on the edge of the filter. When the gasket is worn out, the pot is no longer airtight. This makes it hard during the brewing process to reach the right level of pressure needed to make the coffee come up letting out steam. This will ultimately leave you with little coffee in the collection chamber. Changing the gasket might seem easy, but when the rubber is worn out it might prove rather tricky. Nowadays alongside rubber gaskets you can also find Teflon gaskets that provide a much better seal, and that most importantly are resistant to heat (and that's good when you forget the moka pot on the fire) and in general last much longer.
- handle: its shape and position are important to avoid burning your fingers when you touch it and to provide an easy steady grip of the pot. Another aspect you want to consider is how the handle is mounted onto the pot. The handle is in fact the part of the pot that is most liable to being ruined by a high flame or because the pot is left too long on the heat. If the handle is fixed with screws it is easily replaceable, otherwise once it is ruined it is very hard to repair.

MOKA POT: DIFFERENT SHAPES AND PERFORMANCE

The moka method is definitely a brilliant one and its success has led manufacturers to produce countless versions of it to meet different needs: there are moka pots that make half a cup of coffee and there are models that can brew up to 18.

There are even super-size demonstration moka pots that can brew 50 cups. Considering the complexity of this coffee-maker (see the specific paragraph), the change in scale (miniature or giant size) is not always straightforward. This means that even maintaining a constant volume and design ratio the result may vary. The size that assures the highest result in terms of performance normally is the three-cup moka pot, but some manufacturers, through careful studies on the kinetics of the process, have been able to size the smaller and larger models in order to minimize the difference, so much so that it is even imperceptible to scientific sensory analysis tests.

The filter typically contains 0.1 oz (5 g) of coffee powder per cup, but there are ways of using up to 0.4 oz (13 g) of ground coffee for one or two cups, delivering a higher result in terms of sensory performance.

HOW TO USE A MOKA POT AT ITS BEST

When asked what he thought was the most difficult dish, a great cook once answered that dish was fried eggs. We do not know if this is a true story, but what is certain is that the easier things are, the more details make all the difference.

Thus, making a cup of coffee with a moka pot is one of the easiest things one can do in the kitchen, but brewing a "great cup of coffee" with a moka pot takes some skill. Where to start? The obvious answer would be to start from good quality coffee powder, because if the coffee is not good and not suitable for the moka pot, no matter how hard you try the result won't be up to standard. But we'll talk about this in the next part of the chapter. So let's say we have a fine moka pot, a heat source, some coffee and water. First you must rinse every part of the coffee pot well: the funnel filter, the upper filter (where the gasket is), the upper collection chamber and the lower chamber. Then you pour water inside the lower chamber up to the valve or to the notch (some moka pots have it). If you follow this rule, and if the moka pot is well designed, you'll need about 1.6 fl oz (50 ml) of water for every cup of coffee.

Now you can place the filter on top of the lower chamber, and here comes the hardest part: putting the coffee in. If the powder is in a soft packet, the best thing to do would be simply to pour it directly into the filter creating a mound of powder with the point of this mound well above the edge of the filter. The next step is to gently tap the pot so that the coffee mound gradually levels with the filter. Then you must remove any coffee powder from the edge of the filter and of the lower chamber (with heat that powder might cause the brewed coffee to taste burnt and also reduce the pressure in the chamber ruining the final result, as well as the gasket). Finally screw on the top part to close the moka pot.

If instead you are taking the coffee powder from a jar, you should use a suitably sized spoon, but in some cases it might be necessary to press the coffee into the filter. Keep in mind that our aim is to obtain a perfectly even level of coffee, without any thicker or thinner areas that would make the water pass only in certain areas causing part of the coffee powder to be over extracted in some areas and under extracted in others: a circumstance that would surely spoil your cup of coffee. This is the reason why making the famous three holes with a toothpick is useless and ultimately counterproductive.

So, once the coffee has been placed correctly inside the filter you screw the upper part on and you place the moka on the heat. But what kind of heat? Whatever heat you like. The important thing is that it must be suitable for a moka pot. If it's a gas stove, the flame must not rise above the edge of the pot.

This will stop the handle from burning and, most importantly, will provide a gentle and constant heat to the water that will then push its way through the layer of coffee. Here we need to debunk another myth that says that high flame at the beginning, very low flame at the end is a good thing. If you really want to speed up the operation you can keep a high flame in the first few moments, but then the level of heat must remain constant and not lowered when the first flow of coffee appears. A reduction in heat distribution would cause the water to remain in contact with the coffee powder for too long with the risk of over-extracting unwanted hard woody notes that would badly affect the flavor of the brew.

To keep an eye on the coffee to see when it comes up (moka pots with a transparent lid are perfect in this sense so you can see inside without having to open the pot) is a very good thing, so you can turn off the heat as soon all the coffee has come up. If a moka pot is working correctly, the flow of coffee should be regular until the very end with no gurgling and puffing. At this point keeping the pot on the fire any longer would mean burning it and making its life shorter but also ruining the coffee that you so carefully prepared in the hopes of an excellent result.

The last trick is to give the coffee a gentle stir while still in the moka pot. The different levels of coffee that have collected have a different composition and the brew might not always be homogeneous. Serving the coffee without stirring it first might mean you'll be serving different cups of coffee, especially when using large moka pots, from six cups up.

COFFEE AND THE SENSES: HOW TO ENJOY A GOOD CUP OF COFFEE

COFFEE TASTING: AN ART ACCESSIBLE TO ALL

To those who, for work reasons or for passion, show a deep interest in coffee, a hot cup of coffee may say many things: declare the Coffea species that created the seeds from which that cup of coffee is made, perhaps tell the provenance of the coffee beans, the techniques and technology that were used in the production of the green coffee, the careful selection and mastery in the roasting, and even the level of skill of the person who prepared that single cup. Each of these variables entail a precise blend of the thousands of different molecules contained in the cup of coffee, resulting in the creation of specific combinations – or key sensory points – that can be recognized with our senses through a map that every one of us can create in our own brain.

Coffee tasting is therefore accessible to anyone who wants to learn this art, anyone who is modest enough to never think there is nothing more to learn, anyone who is willing to be guided by those who have made coffee their profession. Our aim however is less ambitious, and we simply set out to provide information that can allow professionals and consumers to outline the sensory profile of the Italian style cup of coffee, to evaluate its hedonic quality and to competently classify what it allows us to decipher through our sense organs. To do this we shall follow the course set out by the International Institute of Coffee Tasters, founded in 1993, with its eleven thousand students in over forty different countries.

COFFEE CUPPING

The procedure for coffee cupping, or coffee tasting is of great importance if we consider the remarkable sensitivity of our sense organs and the power of our brain. Changing the procedure means changing the intensity and even the quality of our perceptions. A cup of coffee held closer to the nose than another offers a different mix of molecules to our sense of smell that must decode it, just as the amount of a sip of coffee can change our perception of the body quality and other parameters of the beverage.

Without wanting to force the coffee tasters to change their habits too much, it is important to acknowledge specific standards and to comply with them during the evaluation. Here follow the steps for a correct cupping procedure.

- STEP 1 - The coffee is served: do not move the cup, observe the color of the cream or of the coffee, the texture of the cream (if there is any cream) and ask yourself how much you like the look of it.

- STEP 2 - Lift the cup to your nose, inhale for about 3 seconds, consider the intensity of the aroma and how pleasant it is.

- STEP 3 - Slurp an about 0.1 fl oz (5 ml) sip of coffee, let it run through your mouth and then swallow it. Consider body, acidity and bitterness.

- STEP 4 - Slurp another 0.1 fl oz (5 ml) sip of coffee, let it run through your mouth, then swallow it keeping your mouth slightly open. Consider all the aftertaste descriptors and, returning to the mouthfeel, consider the astringency.

- STEP 5 - Think about the coffee you have tasted and evaluate it in terms of pleasure: how much pleasure did it give you?

THE ECOSYSTEM FOR COFFEE TASTING

When we talk about sensory analysis nothing more perfect than man exists today, no instrumental equipment has been able to equal man. Unfortunately, man is an extremely complex biological being whose diagnostic capacity and sensitivity are not matched with a brain equally able to memorize and recapture the sensations experienced. To this must be added the fact that the human brain continues to elaborate thoughts and is subject to emotions even when the taster

sets out to carry out a professional sensory analysis. Thoughts and emotions can clearly interfere and influence judgement. This is why it is important to taste when rested, calm and relaxed. Environment is equally important: it should be illuminated by a sufficient amount of natural sunlight (or something similar in quality) and there should be no bad smells or strange odors. Regarding the time of the tasting we must not forget that coffee is enjoyed after a good meal, but if we want to analyze it, the tasting must take place between meals without however the taster feeling very hungry.

CUP OR ESPRESSO CUP?

The size, of course, depends on how much coffee is to be tasted, but in any case shape and size are fundamental for capturing all that coffee has to offer. Let's examine the factors that have led to the creation of the taster's cup for Italian Espresso.

Espresso coffee should be served in an espresso cup. Even if some restaurants try to personalize their service by using larger cups, technically it would be correct to serve the invigorating beverage in 2.5 to 3.3 fl oz (75–100 ml) cups, considering a cup's average volume should be around 0.8 fl oz (25 ml). This type of cup is also suitable for the taster who has to grade a sample, provided the cup complies with the indicated capacity limit, its design adheres to appropriate geometries (a limited diameter keeps the cream together and channels the aroma towards the nose), and that it is made with suitable materials. The cup does in fact influence the visual impact of the cream, has an olfactory influence since it can concentrate or disperse the aromas rising from the beverage, it changes taste perception through the sensation determined by lip contact – especially in terms of heat perception –, and lastly determines the flow of the beverage as it enters the mouth. For all these reasons several studies on the ideal coffee cup have been carried out, studies today have allowed us to outline what the best coffee cup should look like. We have already mentioned the capacity of the cup; as for the materials porcelain is certainly the best as it is remarkably long lasting (unlike earthenware cups it does not chip), has an adequate thermal insulation and a pleasing sensation on lip contact. The ideal geometry should be developed on an ellipse section that narrows but not too much at the top, even if only on the interior, leaving the exterior bell-shaped to facilitate the flow of the beverage into the mouth.

TASTING SPOON

In other coffee cupping techniques, especially those related to the Brazilian method, the equipment includes, among other tools, the so-called goûte caffè, the tasting spoon. This spoon is sometimes asymmetrical, medium sized, wide and shallow, with a relatively long handle. The International Institute of Coffee Tasters however does not adopt this spoon because it does not assure a global sensorial evaluation of the beverage, it entails some practical problems (some tasters do not like to taste from the same cup) and might lead to a misrepresentation of the coffee's characteristics compared to the consumers perception.

COFFEE TEMPERATURE

The sensorial evaluation of a cup of coffee must be carried out when it reaches a temperature of around 149 °F (65 °C). In the case of the espresso, taking into account that once it has reached the cup its temperature is around 176 °F (80 °C), two conditions are necessary for a correct tasting: the sensorial examination must begin within about one minute of the preparation and the cup must be hot, but not boiling hot. As the coffee cools the cream quickly dissolves, a definite weakening of the intensity of the aroma occurs accompanied by a significant change in the olfactory profile and variations in the tactile and taste balance. The same coffee tasted at different temperatures produces differing evaluations.

THE ART OF PERCEPTION AND ITS TOOLS

The environment produces the stimuli that our sensorial system intercepts through the sense organs, each one equipped to detect a particular type of physical or chemical energy.

When the external agent (distal stimulus) makes contact with a receptor, it is transformed into an electrical stimulus (proximal stimulus) through transduction. The new form of energy reaches the brain that decodes and organizes it through basic cognitive processes and dynamic psychological processes: this is perception. Based on this, behavior is organized and a response to the stimulus is achieved.

SENSORIAL EXPLORATION

The pleasure experienced when drinking coffee is greatly increased if a name is given to each perception and if these perceptions are then linked to the origins of the coffee, the methods used to process the green beans, the roasting, and preparation of the beverage. Where to begin? From the sensory exploration. When we taste coffee, our mind generates a unitary perception that is usually expressed with a binary system (yes/no, good/bad) while a trained taster can break down the perception and analyze it.

In this exploration, one that everyone can undertake towards becoming a coffee taster, there are some very useful tools that have been specially developed over the last decades, the latest of which is the coffee tasting map.

Imagine having a cup of coffee in front of you and wanting to record every detail: with the sensory map, tasting becomes a fascinating game that can be played at home or in the coffee shop. Using the map, you learn to explore the very soul of coffee, reaching faraway countries and so increasing the pleasure when drinking it.

Coffee tasting maps also take on a strategic role in the promotion of coffee, in companies, trade shows and other events: coffee from a specific area or a specific company can be characterized with a sensory map that can be used in the tasting, as an informative or decorative element in locations where the product is consumed or sold and it can obviously be used to illustrate the product to consumers during tastings.

SENSORY EVALUATION: THE TASTING CARD

The tasting card is a tool that guides tasters in their sensory evaluation experience and at the same time establishes a unit of measurement for the product's characteristics. In the food sector there are various tasting cards (descriptive, parametric and not, with or without structured scales etc.) and an infinite number of cards can be created depending on the aim of the tasting or on the knowledge of the compiler.

Today, there are many different coffee tasting cards, each with different objectives and levels depending on the organizations that design them. The one we will consider is the recently compiled tasting card of the International Institute of Coffee Tasters, the Trialcard plus, which is extremely practical in its guide to the discovery of coffee.

This tasting card in fact not only includes the classic list of descriptors that indicate the level of pleasure (attractiveness, balance of flavors, tactile balance, delicacy, etc.) but also a series of objective parameters that correspond to specific elements of coffee that are easily related to origin, type of roasting and preparation. Using this card it is possible to identify each coffee and give it a hedonic value according to personal tastes. It also leaves the taster free to add new terms and so make the tasting experience much more personal.

SENSORY EVALUATION

For a taster, as for an attentive consumer, it is fundamental to discover the connections between a perception and the production process, both for the enjoyment and the benefit obtained and because greater knowledge corresponds to greater capacity of memorizing. We shall start, therefore, from the sense organs, from sensory perceptions and their relations with the characteristics of the raw materials and the production techniques.

SIGHT AND VISUAL EVALUATION

Sight is a physical sense organ that gives the perception of the external environment through a form of electromagnetic energy: light.

The sense organ that measures the signals is the sense of sight whose main component is the eye.

Light travels through the cornea and the crystalline lens and reaches the retina where there are two types of sensitive cells:

• cone cells: sensitive to color and details, and are for daytime vision;

• rod cells: these give more approximate vision, they need less energy and are mainly for vision in poor light conditions.

SENSORY MAP OF ESPRESSO COFFEE

Istituto Internazionale
Assaggiatori Caffè

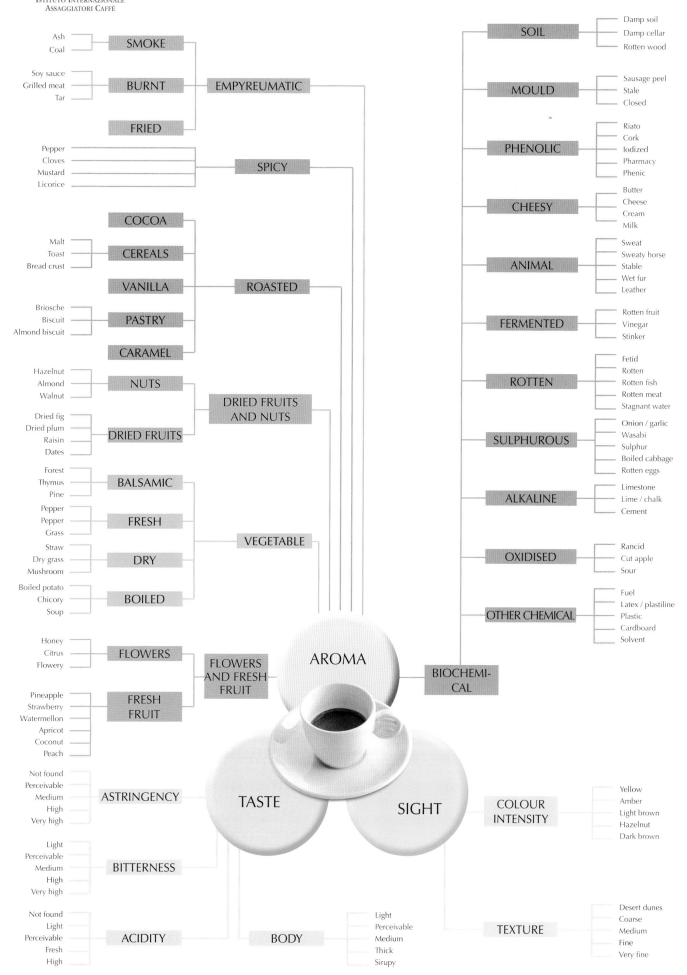

Ash
Coal
— SMOKE

Soy sauce
Grilled meat
Tar
— BURNT — EMPYREUMATIC

FRIED

Pepper
Cloves
Mustard
Licorice
— SPICY

COCOA

Malt
Toast
Bread crust
— CEREALS

VANILLA — ROASTED

Briosche
Biscuit
Almond biscuit
— PASTRY

CARAMEL

Hazelnut
Almond
Walnut
— NUTS

DRIED FRUITS AND NUTS

Dried fig
Dried plum
Raisin
Dates
— DRIED FRUITS

Forest
Thymus
Pine
— BALSAMIC

Pepper
Pepper
Grass
— FRESH

Straw
Dry grass
Mushroom
— DRY — VEGETABLE

Boiled potato
Chicory
Soup
— BOILED

Honey
Citrus
Flowery
— FLOWERS

FLOWERS AND FRESH FRUIT

Pineapple
Strawberry
Watermellon
Apricot
Coconut
Peach
— FRESH FRUIT

AROMA

BIOCHEMI-CAL

SOIL
— Damp soil
— Damp cellar
— Rotten wood

MOULD
— Sausage peel
— Stale
— Closed

PHENOLIC
— Riato
— Cork
— Iodized
— Pharmacy
— Phenic

CHEESY
— Butter
— Cheese
— Cream
— Milk

ANIMAL
— Sweat
— Sweaty horse
— Stable
— Wet fur
— Leather

FERMENTED
— Rotten fruit
— Vinegar
— Stinker

ROTTEN
— Fetid
— Rotten
— Rotten fish
— Rotten meat
— Stagnant water

SULPHUROUS
— Onion / garlic
— Wasabi
— Sulphur
— Boiled cabbage
— Rotten eggs

ALKALINE
— Limestone
— Lime / chalk
— Cement

OXIDISED
— Rancid
— Cut apple
— Sour

OTHER CHEMICAL
— Fuel
— Latex / plastiline
— Plastic
— Cardboard
— Solvent

Not found
Perceivable
Medium
High
Very high
— ASTRINGENCY

Light
Perceivable
Medium
High
Very high
— BITTERNESS

TASTE

SIGHT

COLOUR INTENSITY
— Yellow
— Amber
— Light brown
— Hazelnut
— Dark brown

Not found
Light
Perceivable
Fresh
High
— ACIDITY

BODY
Light
Perceivable
Medium
Thick
Sirupy

TEXTURE
— Desert dunes
— Coarse
— Medium
— Fine
— Very fine

COLOR INTENSITY OF THE CREAM

This is the color saturation level of coffee cream where pale yellow equals zero and monk's tunic brown is the maximum.

The color saturation is stronger in dark roasted Robusta. In the Arabica it is stronger with perfectly mature coffee, rich in sugars and proteins, with a moderate amount of monochloric acids. The roasting level is of course decisive also for Arabica.

TEXTURE OF THE CREAM

If we imagine the cream to be a piece of fabric, irrespective of the quantity and consistency, the texture depends on the density of the weave, the thicker the weave the greater the texture. The maximum level of texture is reached when the weave cannot be perceived because the cream is like colored whipped cream. This parameter can only be used for coffees decorated with cream, a quality that is highly qualifying in Italian Espresso.

Arabica coffee has a very fine texture, especially if it is mature and rich in fats, with a good quantity of sugars and proteins, roasted at the correct slow speed until the beans are fully roasted.

PERSONAL PREFERENCE

This is a hedonic characteristic, basically it determines how inviting the coffee is just by looking at it.

For expert tasters and operators personal preference might decrease when the color is too intense or not intense enough and the texture is loose, which indicates the use of large quantities of dark or light toasted Robusta, of immature beans, careless preparation and so on.

SENSE OF SMELL AND OLFACTORY EVALUATION

Sense of smell is a chemical sense based on the action of receptors located on an about 0.7 square inch (2 square centimeters) mucous membrane placed at the base of the nose. The molecules reach the olfactory epithelium in three ways: orthnasal, retronasal and blood supply. The orthonasal route is direct and begins with the two nostrils and two nasal cavities that are subdivided into three posterior nasal apertures. Along the nasal cavities the air is filtered, moistened and made turbulent by the posterior nasal apertures. The retronasal route starts from the pharynx and communicates with the direct olfactory route to create a genuine draught. The blood supply route is created by the vessels that moisten the olfactory epithelium with blood.

When an active olfactory molecule comes into contact with the olfactory villus the chemical energy is transformed into an electrical signal that, through the olfactory bulb, reaches the brain.

The sense of smell is an incredibly powerful sense:

- it prevails almost completely over the other senses;

- it has an almost infinite range: it has been calculated that it is sensitive to over 400.000 molecules;

- it has a sensitivity that is unequalled by instruments used for chemical research: 1 ppt (1 part on 1.000.000.000.000 parts);

- it is extremely fast: 400 milliseconds;

- it remains vigilant also during sleep;

- it influences directly the right hemisphere of the brain and the limbic system: the location of memory and emotions;

- it also has a subliminal activity, therefore molecules that we do not perceive influence our behavior and our physiology.

Among the general floral notes, the citrusy floral components are often predominant.

There are however some characteristics of the sense of smell that for tasters make it difficult to use, such as its very fast adaptability, its inverse correlation semantics, its emotional effect and its cultural filter.

The olfactory rules for coffee are extremely complex. Over a thousand molecules have been identified with sophisticated instruments that continue to discover more as these instruments are perfected. The activity of these chemical elements depends on their concentration, the relationship between them and on the sensitivity of the taster. This is to say that just one molecule, only in some cases produces a univocal character, in most cases it can indicate many different perceptions.

OLFACTORY INTENSITY

This is the total volume of smells irrespective of their quality and therefore dependent on any raw material and process that results in the creation of strong smelling substances.

Flowers and Fresh Fruit

General floral and citrus notes, honey and general or specific fresh fruit notes.

Floral and fresh fruit notes are mainly related to washed medium to dark roasted Arabica coffee. These notes disappear with strong roasts and are not sufficiently conveyed with light roasting.

Vegetable

Fresh vegetable notes (pea, capsicum, freshly cut grass), dried vegetable notes (straw, hay, mushroom), boiled vegetable notes (potato, chicory) and balsamic vegetable notes (forest, aromatic herbs).

Vegetable notes are stronger in unripe Robusta and Arabica coffee and can peak in coffee with specific defects. Some specific coffee origins, however tend to display particular and rather pleasing vegetable notes.

Nuts and Dried Fruit

Perception of nuts (walnuts, almonds, hazel nuts) and dried fruit (dates, figs, prunes).

This perception is present mainly in washed Arabic coffee, and sometimes in natural slow roasted Arabica coffee.

Vegetable notes may include peas, peppers, grass, leaves, boiled potatoes…

Biscuits, croissant, toasted bread, and caramel are some of the descriptors included in the roasted notes.

Roasted

Perception of cereals (malt, toasted bread, bread crusts), caramel (caramel, burnt sugar), vanilla, cocoa, pastry (croissants, biscuits).

Roasted notes are directly related to the level of the coffee's roasting, some notes such as the natural ones tend to give cocoa and cereal notes. Excessive dark roasting causes the loss of certain notes and the onset of empyreumatic (burnt) notes.

Spice Notes

Perception of spices in general and/or in particular of pepper, cloves, mustard, licorice.

The spice notes are partly linked to the species and origins of the coffee and partly to molecules whose presence is linked to the roasting. The darker the roast the molecules change their aromatic level (passing from dried fruit to roasted).

Empyreumatic

Perception of fried (fried oil), and burnt notes (grilled meat, ash, coal, smoke, burnt rubber).

The empyreumatic notes are directly linked to the type of roasting: even a light, badly performed roasting can give an empyreumatic aroma. Certain types of coffee (Robusta coffees generally) have a greater tendency towards notes of the empyreumatic range.

Other Biochemical Notes

A large category of defects a coffee might have that includes the following notes: earthy, mildew, phenolic, caseous, animal, fermented, putrid, sulfurous, basic, hydrocarbon, oxide and others.

Defects can develop at any stage, but usually they originate from a bad selection of green beans whose defects are then amplified by roasting.

Spicy notes include licorice, pepper, cloves and cinnamon.

Global Positive Notes

The overall intensity of odors originating from good raw materials and a skillfully conducted production process.

Global Negative Notes

The overall intensity of odors originating from damaged raw materials and a faulty production process.

Aroma Persistence

Aroma persistence is the duration of aromas after the beverage has been swallowed. It is evaluated considering only the aromas and not any other sapid or tactile perception.

Aroma persistence is stronger in perfectly roasted mature coffees that have a high level of lipids. Even defective coffees can have great persistence.

Finesse

This is a hedonic descriptor and is therefore subjective. It is used to define the level of elegance and enjoyment of the aroma.

It is at its height in perfectly mature, healthy, skillfully roasted coffee.

Richness

This is a hedonic descriptor and is therefore subjective. It is used to define the complexity of aroma identifying the number of positive notes that can be detected in the evaluated coffee.

Richness is greater in washed coffees, especially if made from mature, healthy, skillfully roasted beans.

Hedonic Level

This is a subjective descriptor measuring the overall pleasantness of the evaluated coffee. It is linked to the quality of the raw material and to a correct production process.

POSTCENTRAL GYRUS SYSTEM AND TACTILE EVALUATION

The postcentral gyrus system is a sensory receptive area of the brain for tactile sensitivity, namely:

- tactile sensitivity

- heat sensitivity

- spain sensitivity

- deep sensitivity (proprioceptors)

- visceral hypersensitivity

Tactile sensitivity has two distinct aspects: on the one hand, it supplies physical perceptions (volume, viscosity, shape, etc.) and on the other, it supplies chemical perceptions. The latter are commonly classified as: astringent (unripe persimmon), pungent (vinegar), hot (chili pepper), metallic (spoon on the tongue) and pseudo-heat (cold like mint, hot like alcohol).

Body

The syrupy level of coffee, otherwise defined as viscosity: filtered coffee has zero body while high extraction espresso coffee has maximum body. Viscosity is higher in well-matured coffee containing fats, rich in sugar and proteins and that has undergone full roasting. Unripe coffee too can deliver a "negative" body quality.

Astringency

Astringency is typically perceived within 15 seconds, manifesting itself through one or more of the following phenomena: altered saliva lubrication, wrinkling and/or xerostomia of the mucous membranes of the mouth.

This perception is usually related to Robusta coffee and immature beans.

Tactile Balance

Tactile balance is given by the spherical perception of the coffee: it is perfect when there are no harsh notes such as astringency and the mucous in the mouth only detects mellowness and silkiness.

Tactile balance is greater in perfectly roasted coffees with few chlorogenic acids and rich in fats and sugars.

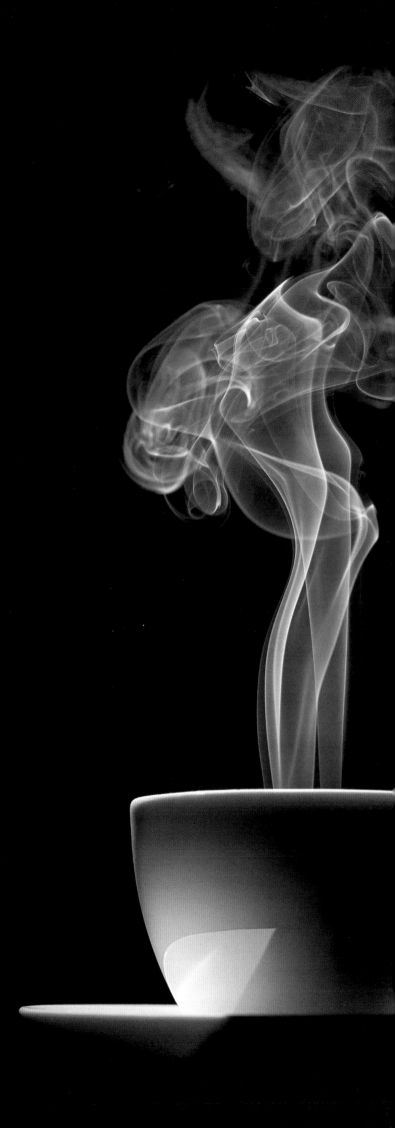

SENSE OF TASTE AND EVALUATION OF FLAVORS

The sense of taste organ is located inside the mouth and identifies the molecules dispersed in a liquid.

Most taste papillae are found on the tongue. Each papilla contains one or more taste buds made of taste cells with microvilli sensitive to substances that have a taste. When one of these substances reaches a microvillus, an electrical signal is triggered that through the taste nerve reaches the brain where it is elaborated.

The coffee taste parameters are relatively simple, but they are extremely important in terms of coffee description because they are easier to interpret than the olfactory notes. After visual evaluation, tastes are in fact the easiest aspects to consider.

Acidity

A sapid perception experienced as a low voltage electrical current across the tongue that disappears very rapidly leaving a fresh sensation.

Acidity is higher in coffee made from immature beans, washed or pulped (descascado) coffees, and in light-roasted coffee.

Bitter

A bitter perception experienced through the taste papillae.

Typically more noticeable in Robusta coffee, immature or defected beans, and in dark roasted coffee.

Flavor Balance

This is a hedonic element, therefore subjective, that considers the balance between acid and bitter. It depends on coffee selection, on the blend's correct combination of natural and washed coffees and balanced roasting.

HOME LESSONS

FOR YOUNG & OLD.

TO SAVE WORRY & WASTE

Go early to bed Drink "Camp" when you rise, & you will be Healthy, Wealthy & Wise.

R. PATERSON & SONS, SOLE PROPRIETORS. GLASGOW.

"CAMP" COFFEE.

Holds the DUX MEDAL
For Purity, Strength & Flavour.
IT HAS NO EQUAL.

COFFEE AND MILK

A PERFECT COMBINATION

Coffee has inspired a great number of brewing and preparation methods: we have described many of them so far but there are also those based on the combination of coffee with other ingredients. Among these ingredients, milk is certainly the most popular. In many countries the milk and coffee combo is almost a must, representing 95% of overall coffee consumption.

CAPPUCCINO

Cappuccino is definitely the most successful milk and coffee drink in the world. Our journey towards making the perfect cappuccino must start with the ingredients and the equipment but will also include the essential manual skills needed towards making a perfect cappuccino. Like in all seemingly simple preparations, every imperfection may lead to a very negative outcome. Learning how to make the perfect cappuccino is not simple, but definitely a very enjoyable challenge.

INGREDIENTS

COFFEE, OR RATHER, CERTIFIED ITALIAN ESPRESSO

If it is true that a drop of good milk can improve a bad coffee, we could also say that defects of a coffee are emphasized in a cappuccino. The reason is simple. Compared to an espresso a cappuccino contains many more fats that bind with every aromatic molecule that are then released in the mouth due to the action of saliva and to the movements of the tongue, thereby activating the olfactory perception. And it is a fact that our sense of smell acts beyond our consciousness, keeping us from eating unpleasant foods even if we cannot identify the reasons.

A poor coffee blend may cause the appearance of additional substances (chlorogenic acid, for example) that can alter the structure of the frothed milk, separating its components, and therefore altering the tactile characteristics of the cappuccino.

The first point to consider therefore is the coffee blend, that must have a strong aromatic expression, with deep tones (rich in positive aromas) and a perfect sensory profile. Bad smelling blends and overly roasted and astringent blends must be avoided.

The second, but not less important aspect to consider, is the preparation of the espresso and its quantity used. Here we repeat the obligatory rule: 0.8 fl oz (25 ml) in 25 seconds. A good cappuccino cannot be made with a lungo espresso coffee (that is an espresso made with more water).

In conclusion: the basis for a perfect cappuccino is a Certified Italian Espresso.

MILK

For cappuccino you need fresh, full fat, top quality milk. Milk is important not only because it makes up most of the volume of a cappuccino but also because of the elements it adds. Fats, about 3.5%, are aroma fixatives in milk and in coffee, but depending on their globular conformation they also have a strong effect on the tactile characteristics: they emphasize the underlying mellowness, the greatly appreciated subtle velvet feel that gives lasting pleasure after the beverage has been swallowed. The proteins (3.2%), through their long-branched chains, allow the milk to be frothed and they are mainly responsible for its creaminess. It goes without saying that the aroma molecules present in the milk blend with those in the coffee to offer complex new aromas and new levels of pleasantness: if the milk undergoes a long heating process, not only the physical structure of certain elements will be altered, but the milk's chemical composition will be altered too, with, for example, an increase of molecules bringing empyreumatic odors. These – and others – sometimes are not perceptible in milk, but they are in a cappuccino, as a result of the synergy with those molecules already present in coffee.

COFFEE AND MILK

Milk must be kept in the fridge at a temperature of 38–41 °F (3–5 °C) and frothed cold: if the frothing operation is correct, 3.3 fl oz (100 ml) of milk should reach the ideal serving temperature (around 131 °F/55 °C), and a volume of 4.2 fl oz (125 ml). The milk when frothed for a cappuccino has a density of about 0.6. If the hot milk from a previous frothing is used again, not only will the operation prove harder but the result will be less creamy, with higher chances of separation of the components and of serving a cappuccino that is too hot.

SECONDARY INGREDIENTS

Cocoa, powdered chocolate and other ingredients: are they really necessary? Far be it from us to limit anyone's imagination, but we strongly believe that the addition of different ingredients other than espresso coffee (therefore including any other type of coffee preparation) and frothed milk leads to different beverages, to more or less successful variations of the classic cappuccino.

EQUIPMENT

DOSER GRINDER AND ESPRESSO MACHINE

A doser grinder and an espresso machine are necessary to make espresso coffee. But an espresso machine also needs to supply the energy necessary for frothing the milk. Frothing is done with a steam wand that has 3, 4 or 5 nozzles on the end. It goes without saying that the machine boiler must assure the right temperature to guarantee the supply of a correct quantity of steam with the correct thermal energy. But an equally important feature to consider is the length of the steam wand: if too short, it won't penetrate correctly into the milk frothing pitcher and the movements necessary to froth the milk will be difficult to carry out. For the same reasons flexibility is also very important.

Regarding the nozzles, some operators recommend the use of wands with four 0.05 in (1.5 mm) diameter holes so that the pressure is sufficiently strong and the temperature does not rise too quickly, avoiding the break-up of the cream making it foamy. Others believe that the choice of the wand should adapt to the barista's manual skill.

MILK PITCHERS

A milk pitcher must be in stainless steel, and must comply with specific design standards. A barista should also have at hand three different size pitchers.

Stainless steel (ideally 18/10 grade) is a metal that transmits heat easily and allows a simple monitoring of the temperature with the palm of the hand. Other pros of stainless steel are that it is easy to clean, it is resistant, and aesthetically pleasing. Porcelain is not recommended due to its insulation and fragility.

The design of a milk pitcher is always circular and must be narrower at the top and have a spout, necessary for creating decorated cappuccinos. The swelling in the lower part favors a type of movement in the milk that allows it to blend with steam and create a very creamy liquid that won't tend to separate.

The recommended capacities are 16, 23, and 33 fl oz (0.5, 0.75, 1 l) for the preparation of respectively two, three and four cappuccinos at a time without ever having any milk left to heat again. Another important rule to follow is that a milk pitcher should never be more than half filled.

CAPPUCCINO CUP

If the espresso cup is so important that the International Institute of Coffee Tasters has provided a rigorous definition of this objet in terms of material, shape and size, the same should be said for the cappuccino cup whose ideal format should also be defined.

The best material for a cappuccino cup is white feldspathic porcelain: this elegant material does not interfere with the visual aspect of the cappuccino and also highlights the qualities of a well prepared cappuccino.

The ideal capacity of a cappuccino cup is 5.5 fl oz (165 ml), more or less 10%, that is between 5 and 6 fl oz (150–180 ml) composed of 0.8 fl oz (25 ml) of espresso and 3.3 fl oz (100 ml) of frothed milk (that rises to a volume of about 4.2 fl oz/125 ml). The cappuccino must be served in a full cup with the frothy layer clearly visible.

If material and capacity are important, so is design, because it is precisely during the pouring of the frothed milk that the coffee is incorporated into the milk and that the perfect ring that decorates the surface of the classic cappuccino is created. The base of the cup must therefore be oval, with differentiated levels of thickness. The cup must have a suitable diameter, with a rim that is thin enough to avoid the consumer thinking it is a cheaply made cup.

METHOD FOR PREPARING A CAPPUCCINO

FROTHING THE MILK

Half fill an adequately sized milk pitcher with milk from the fridge at a temperature of 38–41 °F (3–5 °C).

Turn on the steam to eliminate any condensation in the wand, and at this point start frothing the milk. Various techniques can be used depending on a variety of factors: volume of steam, level of wand immersion in the milk, angle of immersion in respect of the vertical position of the milk pitcher, and movements of the latter. Some baristas recommend immersing the wand half way down the milk level, give maximum steam, and then immediately bring the nozzle up almost to the surface of the milk, and finally plunge it down again and so end the operation. Others prefer to keep the nozzle near the surface of the milk right from the beginning, recommending not to place it in the center but near the brim at a suitable angle that will produce a consistent swirling movement in the milk. To finish, a brief plunge of the nozzle to almost the bottom of the milk pitcher.

The fact remains that every technique can be considered valid if it results in a uniform "cream" without bubbles. In this phase, the sense of hearing can be helpful: hissing and gurgling sounds can be important to understand how the operation is going and at what point it is.

ADDING THE MILK TO THE COFFEE

If milk is frothed correctly it will not separate easily, therefore there is no need to use it too quickly. In fact, a short pause is good for frothed milk: it becomes smoother and the foam bubbles that form on the surface burst, so it is not necessary to tap the milk pitcher on the counter something professional baristas consider to be deplorable.

Therefore, there is plenty of time to take the cup in one hand and the milk pitcher in the other. For a classic cappuccino, the pitcher should be brought very close to the cup and the frothed milk made to slide down the side so that the coffee can form the typical brown border. For a decorated cappuccino, the frothed milk is poured into the center, first with the nozzle close to the coffee, then moving away working skillfully with the wrist of the hand holding the pitcher to create the required design.

It is important to ask if the customer wants cocoa before adding the milk and if so sprinkle it over the coffee. The same should apply to sugar: some baristas sugar the coffee to allow the customer to drink the cappuccino as it is served, without the overall appearance being ruined by stirring.

SERVING COFFEE
A skillful barista serves a cappuccino without spilling any of the cream. The worst thing for a customer would be to have some of the cappuccino in the saucer, making it difficult to drink the beverage without getting dirty. Timing is of great importance when serving a cappuccino: it should be consumed within 30 seconds of its preparation, purists say. However, any pause can jeopardize the result, including the temperature, which is very important for the first olfactory impression but also for the following heat perception. If a cold cappuccino is not enjoyable, a boiling hot cappuccino isn't either causing the consumer to take little sips reducing the overall pleasantness of the experience.

COFFEE AND MILK

MACCHIATO COFFEE
SERVES 4

INGREDIENTS
4 CUPS OF ESPRESSO COFFEE
1.3 FL OZ (40 ML) FRESH FULL FAT MILK

PREPARATION

Add about 0.3 fl oz (10 ml) of milk to a cup of espresso. There are three options: the milk can be either cold, hot, or even frothed as for cappuccino.

The original recipe does not include any addition, but a macchiato can be served with a cocoa or cinnamon powder decoration to make the beverage more delicious.

COFFEE AFFOGATO (DROWNED IN COFFEE)
SERVES 4

INGREDIENTS
4 TSP INSTANT COFFEE
2 TSP SUGAR
CREAM, PISTACHIO OR CINNAMON GELATO TO TASTE

PREPARATION

Pour 4 demicups of hot water with the instant coffee and the sugar in a cocktail shaker or a glass jar.
Close the lid and shake vigorously to make a 0.3 in (1 cm) froth on the surface.
Taste the dessert and add another tsp of sugar if the result is not sweet enough, but consider that the gelato will also increase the sweetness.
Add 2 scoops of gelato in each cup and pour the coffee over it while still hot.
Serve straight away.

Coffee affogato, literally "drowned in coffee," is a delicious, tasty and refreshing dessert, the perfect conclusion to a summer or even winter meal. You can make affogato with any type of cream gelato, apart from strong-tasting chocolate gelato. Stracciatella (chocolate chip) gelato is also a good option, with its small chocolate shavings delicately complementing the flavor of the coffee without altering it.

LICORICE WHITE
SERVES 4

INGREDIENTS
3.3-4 FL OZ (100-120 ML) LUNGO ESPRESSO COFFEE
1.4 OZ (40 G) WHITE CHOCOLATE
4 TSP LICORICE
0.6 FL OZ (20 ML) LIQUID SUGAR
20 CRUSHED ICE CUBES

PREPARATION

Make the espresso, heat 4 glasses or tall cups and keep them warm, for example placing them in a bain-marie keeping them away from the flame. The inside of the cups must remain dry.
Chop the white chocolate into tiny pieces and place them in a glass to melt.
Do the same with the licorice.
Pour the melted white chocolate in the heated cups or glasses. Then add the licorice on top creating two different color levels.
Pour the ice, the liquid sugar and half of the coffee into a frothing jug. Whisk the ingredients with a milk frother or a whisk until a soft froth is formed.
Pour the remaining coffee over the layers of chocolate and licorice and delicately top with the froth and serve.

This unique beverage will surprise you with its mosaic of different flavors: the richness coffee, the sweet mellowness of white chocolate, and the fragrant vibrancy of licorice.

COFFEE AND MILK

CAFFELATTE
SERVES 4

INGREDIENTS
4 FL OZ (120 ML) ESPRESSO COFFEE
• 27 FL OZ (800 ML) FULL FAT FRESH MILK • SUGAR TO TASTE

PREPARATION

Heat the milk in a suitably sized jug.
Make espresso coffee using a moka pot or coffee pods.
Pour the milk into four cups and then add the coffee.
Add sugar to taste and serve.

Caffelatte is the typical breakfast beverage, a ritual to kick off the day loved by children and grownups alike. Unlike cappuccino, caffelatte does not have the froth and it usually comes in larger servings. Perfect for dunking cookies, cereals, and fibers.

COFFEE MILK SHAKE
SERVES 4

INGREDIENTS
10 OZ (300 G) OF EITHER COFFEE, CREAM OR VANILLA GELATO •
1.6 FL OZ (50 ML) COLD COFFEE • 12 CRUSHED ICE CUBES •
2 TBSP SUGAR • 16.9 FL OZ (0.5 L) FRESH MILK

PREPARATION

Crush the ice and place it in the mixer. Add the cold coffee, milk, gelato and sugar.
Mix for about 3 minutes until frothy.
Pour into the single glasses and serve.

A coffee milk shake is a classic summer drink: fresh, tasty and irresistible. Easy to prepare, you can also make it with leftover coffee or by replacing the gelato with 3.3 fl oz (100 ml) of very cold whipping cream.

LATTE MACCHIATO THE GERMAN WAY
SERVES 4

INGREDIENTS
4 CUPS OF ESPRESSO COFFEE • 4 GLASSES OF FRESH MILK

PREPARATION

Heat the milk without bringing it to a boil.
Froth half of the milk until you obtain a soft frothy texture.
Pour some of the froth into a glass while making it swirl. Leave it to cool down.
Add the hot milk.
Make the espresso coffees and pour them over the milk mixing well.
Top with the remaining froth.

LATTE MACCHIATO (COFFEE-STAINED MILK)
SERVES 4

INGREDIENTS
4 CUPS OF ESPRESSO COFFEE • 4 GLASSES OF FRESH MILK •
SUGAR AND EXTRACTS (VANILLA, ALMOND) TO TASTE

PREPARATION

Heat the milk without bringing it to a boil.
Froth some of the milk until you get a soft cream. Add the sugar
or the extracts to taste and set aside.
Pour the milk into a tall tumbler making it quickly swirl and leave it to cool a little.
Make the cups of espresso coffee and pour them slowly into the milk,
stirring well. Incorporate the froth you had set aside.
If you are feeling creative, you can add a few drops of coffee on top to create a
decoration using any sharp kitchen implement.

Latte macchiato basically inverts the coffee/milk ratio of caffè macchiato.
Latte macchiato is a way of quenching your need of coffee, allowing you
to enjoy perhaps another espresso during the day.

MAROCCHINO COFFEE
SERVES 4

INGREDIENTS
3.3 FL OZ (100 ML) ESPRESSO COFFEE
2 FL OZ (60 ML) HOT CHOCOLATE
3.3 FL OZ (100 ML) FRESH FULL FAT MILK
COCOA POWDER TO TASTE
SUGAR TO TASTE

PREPARATION

Let the hot chocolate cool down and pour it into the glasses.
Heat the milk without bringing it to a boil.
Make the espresso coffee, pour it over the hot chocolate and sprinkle a little cocoa powder on top.
Froth the milk in a jug using a milk frother or a mixer, add it to the coffee, sprinkle a little more cocoa powder and serve.
You can also froth the milk with an espresso machine steam wand. If you prefer a slightly sweeter dessert add a few teaspoons of sugar and stir.

A cup of Marocchino coffee is also a visual experience. This beverage is typically served in a transparent cup that lets you see the different layers and anticipate their flavors: the chocolate base, the coffee with its cocoa powder topping, and the final milk froth layer chromatically and deliciously crowning the composition.

COFFEE AND MILK

TURKISH COFFEE
SERVES 4

INGREDIENTS
6.7 FL OZ (200 ML) OF WATER
5 TSP OF COFFEE POWDER
SUGAR TO TASTE
CARDAMOM, CINNAMON OR NUTMEG TO TASTE

PREPARATION

To make a good Turkish coffee it is best to start from Arabica coffee beans grinding them with a grinding machine or with pestle and mortar, until you obtain a powder as fine as cocoa powder.

This will bring out the true aroma of freshly ground coffee and make you fully enjoy the preparation process.

Pour the water in the cezve (approximately 1.6 fl oz/ 50 ml per cup). Add the sugar and the spices, and stir well.

Add 1 tsp of coffee for each person plus one.

Place the cezve on a gentle heat and bring to a boil being careful not to spill the foam that will form.

Remove from the heat and pour half a cup of coffee and a little froth in each cup.

Return the cezve to the heat and when the coffee comes to the boil again, fill up the cups, pouring the coffee laterally in order to maintain the froth.

Before serving, add one tbsp of cold water to make the coffee powder settle at the bottom of the cup.

Turkish coffee is the essence of Turkish culture, the embodiment of the sense of hospitality of a country that has always been a bridge between east and west. Turkish coffee is an everyday beverage that is also served on important family life occasions: when a young man and his father visit a girl's parents to ask for her hand, cups of coffee are served before the conversation starts. Coffee made the Turkish way is actually common across all middle-eastern countries and in Greece. To prepare this type of coffee you need the special copper and brass long-handled jug called cezve.

BICERIN

SERVES 6

INGREDIENTS

6.7 FL OZ (200 ML) ESPRESSO COFFEE
2 TBS OF SUGAR
7 OZ (200 G) DARK CHOCOLATE
1.6 FL OZ (50 ML) FRESH WHIPPING CREAM
1.6 FL OZ (50 ML) MILK

PREPARATION

Make the espresso coffee using a high quality blend. Add some sugar and keep warm.

Melt and stir the sugar over a gentle heat to obtain a syrup.

Place the whipping cream with the syrup obtained from the sugar in a bowl and whisk manually until you obtain a semi-firm, soft, velvety texture.

Finely chop the chocolate and melt it in a bain-marie or in the microwave.

Slowly add part of the milk and the whipped cream (keeping some aside) and stir and blend well.

Add a little chocolate to the leftover whipping cream. Stir them together and leave aside.

Fill half of each bicerin with the chocolate. Pour the coffee on top of the chocolate and stir well to blend all the flavors. Top with the cream and chocolate up to the brim of the cup.

Serve hot and enjoy.

Bicerin, literally "small glass" in the dialect of Piedmont, is a typical non-alcoholic drink of Turin deriving from the recipe of the so-called "bavareisa," an eighteenth-century beverage made with coffee, chocolate and frothed milk or whipping cream. Bicerin is a delicious treat combining the flavor of coffee, chocolate and milk for a truly flavorsome result.

COFFEE À LA RUSSE
SERVES 4

INGREDIENTS
4 CUPS OF HOT COFFEE • 8 TBSP OF COFFEE LIQUOR •
6.7 FL OZ (2 DL) VODKA • SUGAR TO TASTE

PREPARATION

Prepare the coffee and pour it into the glasses. In every glass, add sugar to taste
and 2 tbsp of coffee liquor.
Add the vodka, stir and serve.

*Due to its alcoholic content, this beverage is better served during the winter.
It can also be made thicker by adding a little condensed milk that must
be stirred in well at the end of the preparation.*

THE SULTAN'S COFFEE
SERVES 4

INGREDIENTS
27 FL OZ (8 DL) BOILING COFFEE • 4.5 OZ (130 G) DARK CHOCOLATE •
SUGAR OR HONEY TO TASTE • 12 TBSP OF WHIPPING CREAM •
CINNAMON POWDER OR ORANGE ZEST

PREPARATION

Break up the chocolate and leave it to melt in a bain-marie.
Add sugar to taste and stir it in, then pour into four transparent glasses.
Whisk half of the coffee until frothy and leave aside.
Pour a little whipping cream in each glass, then slowly pour
in the liquid coffee and its froth.
Whip the remaining cream until stiff and add some to each glass.
Top with a sprinkle of cinnamon.

CUBAN COFFEE
SERVES 2

INGREDIENTS
1 TSP OF BROWN SUGAR • 2.5 TSP OF COFFEE POWDER • 0.6 FL OZ (20 ML) DARK CUBAN RUM •
1 STRIP OF LEMON ZEST

PREPARATION

Prepare the moka pot putting the water in the lower chamber.
Mix the sugar and the coffee powder together and put the mix
into the filter without pressing. Place the moka over a gentle heat
and remove as soon as the coffee has come up.
Pour into the coffee cups and add the rum. Decorate with lemon zest
and enjoy the fabulous aroma.

Cuban coffee is a beverage characterized by a unique, intense,
sweet taste deriving from the brown sugar and the rum. The ideal coffee
for this recipe would obviously be Cuban coffee, but any Arabica will do.

MEXICAN COFFEE
SERVES 4

INGREDIENTS
1.6 FL OZ (50 ML) DOUBLE CREAM • 0.1 OZ (4 G) CINNAMON • A PINCH (1 G) NUT MEG •
0.5 OZ (15 G) SUGAR • 2 ½ CUPS OF BOILING HOT COFFEE • 8 TSP OF CHOCOLATE SYRUP

PREPARATION

Pour the double cream into a bowl and mix it with 1/3 of the cinnamon.
Add the nutmeg, sugar, and whisk until rather thick.
Prepare the base putting 2 tsp of chocolate syrup in each glass.
Add the coffee, stir well to blend the flavors.
Add the leftover cinnamon to the whipped cream and pour into the glasses.

PARISIAN COFFEE
SERVES 2

INGREDIENTS
2 DEMITASSES OF STRONG COFFEE • 1 DEMITASSES OF HOT CHOCOLATE •
2 TSP COGNAC • SUGAR TO TASTE • 1 FL OZ (30 ML) WHIPPED CREAM

PREPARATION

Pour ¾ of the coffee and an equal amount of hot chocolate into
two small glass cups and stir. Add the cognac and the sugar to taste,
then incorporate the remaining coffee mixed with a little whipped cream.
Pour into the cups and serve adding a few teaspoons of whipped cream.

SHAKERATO COFFEE
SERVES 2

INGREDIENTS
4 CUPS OF STRONG ESPRESSO • 2 TBSP CRUSHED ICE •
2 TSP SUGAR SYRUP

PREPARATION

Pour the coffee, the syrup and the crushed ice into a shaker.
Shake vigorously for at least one minute and serve in ice-cold glasses.

*Shakerato coffee is a delicious summer drink, a pleasant and refreshing break
during the hot hours of the day.*

VALDOSTANO COFFEE
SERVES 6

INGREDIENTS
6 CUPS OF STRONG COFFEE
6 SHOT GLASSES OF GRAPPA
6 SHOT GLASSES OF RED WINE
2 SHOT GLASSES OF GENEPÌ LIQUOR
1 ORGANIC LEMON ZEST
12 TSP OF SUGAR

PREPARATION

Put the sugar in the grole and add the hot coffee, the grappa, the red wine, the genepì and the grated lemon zest.

Heat the grole bain-marie or use steam from an espresso machine. When hot, sprinkle the spouts with some sugar that with the heat will caramelize acquiring a special flavor.

The grole is passed to every member of the group who must take a sip of Valdostano coffee from their spout. The quantity should allow for several turns.

Groles are made for drinking with friends, since in Val D'Aosta they say that who drinks alone will choke.

Valdostano coffee (literally "coffee of the Val D'Aosta region") requires a grole or coupe de l'amitié, that is a carved wooden bowl with four spouts, typically used to drink coffee with a group of friends underlining the value of friendship and community living.

VIENNESE COFFEE
SERVES 4

INGREDIENTS
3.5 OZ (100 G) DARK CHOCOLATE • 4 TBSP WHIPPING CREAM •
2 ½ CUPS OF BOILING HOT COFFEE • 5 FL OZ (150 ML) DOUBLE CREAM •
1 TSP SUGAR

PREPARATION

Melt the chocolate in a small pot and pour it into four hot glasses.
Slowly add the coffee and the tablespoons of whipping cream,
whisking well until frothy and keep warm.
Whip the double cream and sugar and garnish by adding a few
tablespoons of whipped double cream to each glass.

MARTINI COFFEE
SERVES 4

INGREDIENTS
4 CUPS OF STRONG ESPRESSO • 4 TBSP OF SUGAR
• 4 FL OZ (120 ML) VODKA • SOME CRUSHED ICE •
FINELY GRATED CHOCOLATE

PREPARATION

Pour coffee, sugar, vodka and ice into the shaker. Shake well.
Filter and pour into each glass. Garnish with a sprinkle of grated chocolate.

COFFEE AND MILK

EXTRA STRONG COFFEE GRANITA
SERVES 2

INGREDIENTS
4 CUPS STRONG COFFEE
2 CUPS SUGAR
2 GLASSES KAHLÚA (MEXICAN COFFEE LIQUOR)
2 GLASSES DARK RUM
2 CUPS CRUSHED ICE
8 TBSP HONEY

PREPARATION

Mix sugar, honey, and the liquors in a metal container. Add the cold coffee and place in the freezer for one hour.
Scrape the icy mixture with a fork to make granita.
Add the crushed ice and return to the freezer for other 3 hours, scraping the mixture every hour.
Place the granita in the serving glasses and enjoy.

COFFEE AND MILK

COFFEE GROG
SERVES 4

INGREDIENTS
12 LUMPS OF SUGAR • 4 STRIPS OF ORGANIC LEMON ZEST • 4 TBSP OF BRANDY
(FOR FLAMBÉING) • 4 CUPS ESPRESSO COFFEE

PREPARATION

Rinse 4 glasses with hot water. Place 4 lumps of sugar in every glass
and add the lemon zest.
Add the coffee. Flame the tablespoons of brandy with a lighter and
add them to the coffee. Serve while still very hot.

*The name Grog derives from gros grain the coarse wool-and-silk fabric worn
by British admiral Edward Vernon who went down in history for having
prohibited spirits to his crew. The only drink they were allowed was watered
down rum to keep them from getting drunk.*

IRISH COFFEE
SERVES 4

INGREDIENTS
4 FL OZ (120 ML) IRISH WHISKEY • 0.5 OZ (15 G) BROWN SUGAR •
10 FL OZ (300 ML) STRONG COFFEE • 1.5 FL OZ (45 ML)
DOUBLE CREAM, LIGHTLY WHIPPED

PREPARATION

Heat 4 glass cups or 4 tall glasses. Dry them inside and pour in the sugar.
Add the whiskey and then the coffee.
Stir well until sugar dissolves. Then add a spoonful of cream and stir.

COFFEE SORBET
SERVES 4

INGREDIENTS
14 OZ (400 G) SUGAR
8.8 OZ (250 G) STRONG COFFEE
8.4 FL OZ (250 ML) WATER
1 EGG WHITE
A LITTLE COFFEE POWDER

PREPARATION

Add 12 oz (350 g) of sugar to the water. Place over the heat
and boil for one minute.

Add the coffee and stir well using a whisk.

Place in the fridge to cool for a few hours and then pour in
a metal vessel, filtering with a small colander.

Beat the egg white and the rest of the sugar until stiff and
delicately add it to the mixture.

Place in the freezer for about 6 hours and use a mixer or a
whisk to stir it around two or three times so that it remains
homogeneous.

Leave out of the freezer for about 10 minutes before serving.

Serve in tall thin glasses and sprinkle with a little coffee
powder.

COFFEE AND MILK

20 RECIPES

BY CHEF GIOVANNI RUGGIERI

PAIRING
COFFEE AND FOOD

BEETROOT AND COFFEE SCALLOPS WITH A CHILI AND DARK COCOA SAUCE

SERVES 4

12 SCALLOPS
1 OZ (30 G) CLARIFIED BUTTER
3.5 OZ (100 G) VACUUM PACKED COOKED BEETROOT
0.7 OZ (20 G) EXTRA VIRGIN OLIVE OIL
0.1 OZ (4 G) COFFEE POWDER
0.2 OZ (8 G) COCOA POWDER
3.5 OZ (100 G) CHOPPED TOMATOES
1 SHALLOT
0.1 OZ (5 G) CONCENTRATED TOMATO PUREE
0.3 OZ (10 G) WHITE VINEGAR
1 OZ (30 G) CASTER SUGAR
0.1 OZ (5 G) SOY SAUCE
3 RED HOT CHILI PEPPERS
0.7 OZ (20 G) SESAME OIL
SALT TO TASTE

PREPARATION TIME: 30 MINUTES

Julienne the chili peppers and the shallot and brown them in the sesame oil. Add the concentrated tomato puree, chopped tomatoes, a little salt, soy sauce, vinegar, sugar and cook for about 1 hour on a gentle heat until you obtain a thick sauce. Mix it to make it nice and smooth and leave to cool. Filter with a colander.

Peel the beetroot and mix it adding 1.7 oz (50 g), olive oil and a pinch of salt. Keep the cream warm in a bain-marie.

Using a spoon separate the scallops from the shells. Rinse them under running water, delicately remove the coral pulp and the stomach. Dry on some absorbent paper, transfer onto a plate and sprinkle some salt on top. Put the butter in a pan over a high heat and brown three scallops at a time on each side, so that the cooking temperature remains constant. Rapidly brown the coral pulp too (2 minutes).

Irregularly display the beetroot cream and the chili sauce, adding the scallops and sprinkling the coffee and cocoa powder on top. Serve hot.

BRAISED ARTICHOKES AND JERUSALEM ARTICHOKES CREAMED WITH PARMIGIANO REGGIANO CHEESE WITH A TOUCH OF COFFEE

SERVES 4

4 ARTICHOKES
4 MEDIUM-SIZE JERUSALEM ARTICHOKFS
1 LEMON
0.3 FL OZ (10 ML) WHITE WINE
0.3 OZ (10 G) WHITE VINEGAR
10.5 OZ (300 G) GRATED PARMIGIANO
REGGIANO CHEESE
3.5 OZ (100 G) WHIPPING CREAM

10.5 OZ (300 G) MILK
1 OZ (30 G) ESPRESSO COFFEE
0.3 OZ (9 G) AGAR-AGAR
2.4 OZ (70 G) BUTTER
0.3 OZ (9 G) UNREFINED BROWN SUGAR
SALT AND PEPPER TO TASTE
EXTRA VIRGIN OLIVE OIL TO TASTE
COFFEE POWDER TO GARNISH

PREPARATION TIME: 1 HOUR

Place a bain-marie pot over a gentle heat. Pour in the cream, butter and Parmigiano Reggiano cheese until you obtain a fondue. Then use an immersion blender to make the cream perfectly smooth.

Pour the milk in equal quantities into three different pots. In each pot add a different quantity of coffee: 0.1 oz (5 g) in the first, 0.3 oz (10 g) in the second, and 0.5 oz (15 g) in the third. Add the sugar, stir and bring to a boil. Leave to cool, add 0.1 oz (3 g) of agar-agar in each pot, whisk and bring to a boil. Leave to cool for 3 hours until the sauces become firm.

Use an immersion blender to mix them into a fluid cream.

Remove the artichokes' hard outer leaves, trim the thorny tips and peel the stalks. Cut the artichokes in half, remove the choke with a small knife and place in a bowl of cold water with some lemon juice. Peel the Jerusalem artichokes and add them to the lemony water too.

Fill a saucepan with enough water to cook the Jerusalem artichokes, add salt and the vinegar and cook over a gentle heat until soft, but not overcooked. Drain the Jerusalem artichokes, cut the ends and use a ring mold to shape them into small cylinders. Cut them into approximately 0.7 in (2 cm) discs.

Pour some oil in a non-stick pan and stir fry the artichokes for 3 minutes over a high heat. Add salt and pepper, add the wine and let it evaporate. Then put the lid on and leave to cook until all the liquid has evaporated.

Place the three coffee sauces on the plate, put the hot vegetables on top and pour over the hot Parmigiano Reggiano fondue. Garnish with coffee powder before serving.

COFFEE-SMOKED VEAL FILLET WITH COCOA BEAN IN BALSAMIC VINEGAR SWEET-AND-SOUR SAUCE AND SWEET POTATO CHIPS

SERVES 4

14 OZ (400 G) VEAL FILLET
3.5 OZ (100 G) COFFEE BEANS
3.5 OZ (100 G) BEECH WOOD CHIPS FOR SMOKING
1 COCOA BEAN
2 ORANGE SWEET POTATOES
13.5 FL OZ (400 ML) CORN OIL FOR FRYING
5.2 OZ (150 G) BALSAMIC VINEGAR
1.7 OZ (50 G) UNREFINED BROWN SUGAR
10 BLACK PEPPERCORNS
SALT AND PEPPER TO TASTE
EXTRA VIRGIN OLIVE OIL TO TASTE

PREPARATION TIME: 45 MINUTES

Preheat the oven to 195 °F (90 °C). Place the smoking wood chips in a 5.9 in (15 cm) non-stick pan with a steam-cooking grill. Set the wood chips alight until they burn completely, then sprinkle the coffee beans on top. Place the fillet on the grill, cover it with the lid and place in the oven for 30 minutes. Brush the meat with olive oil letting it brown on both sides in the non-stick pan and grate the cocoa bean while turning the meat on both sides. Add salt and pepper.

Pour vinegar, sugar, and pepper in a pot, and place over a gentle heat until they thicken into a sauce. Remove the peppercorns using a colander.

Heat the corn oil in a deep frying pan. Wash and dry the potatoes. With a mandoline slicer cut them into about 1mm slices. Fry the potatoes in the hot oil without letting the slices overlap. Shake the pan so that the slices fry evenly. When ready remove the chips from the pan and transfer them onto some absorbent paper. Add other potatoes to the oil. Continue like this until all the potatoes are ready.

Cut the fillet into 4 slices and place each slice onto the plates. Pour some sweet-and-sour sauce, add a few chips on the side and serve.

BUTTER AND TARRAGON ESCARGOTS WITH COFFEE AND JUNIPER SAUCE

SERVES 4

24 LUMACHE
24 ESCARGOTS
5.6 OZ (160 G) BUTTER
1.4 OZ (40 G) BREAD CRUMBS
0.3 OZ (10 G) TARRAGON
1.6 FL OZ (50 ML) WHITE WINE
1 OZ (30 G) WHITE VINEGAR
1 GARLIC CLOVE
1 OZ (30 G) SODIUM BICARBONATE TO CLEANSE
THE ESCARGOT SHELLS
SALT AND PEPPER TO TASTE
WATERCRESS SPROUTS TO HAVE ON THE SIDE

FOR THE SAUCE:
1 CELERY STALK • 1 CARROT • 1 ONION •
1 TSP OF TOMATO CONCENTRATE • 1 VEAL
KNEE • 2 PEPPERCORNS • 1 SMALL BAY
LEAF • 3.3 FL OZ (100 ML) WHITE WINE •
0.1 OZ (5 G) POTATO STARCH •
1 OZ (30 G) CRUSHED COFFEE BEANS •
2 CRUSHED JUNIPER BERRIES • EXTRA VIRGIN
OLIVE OIL TO TASTE

PREPARATION TIME, COOKING EXCLUDED: 1 HOUR (at least)

Preheat the oven to 390 °F (200 °C), grease the veal knee and place in the oven for about 30 minutes until it becomes brown.

Wash the vegetables, dice them and brown them in a pan with a little oil. Place the vegetables in a large saucepan, add the knee, the tomato concentrate, the bay leaves, the peppercorns. Pour in the wine and simmer until it evaporates. Add some cold water and a few ice cubes filling the saucepan up to the brim and bring to a boil over a gentle heat. Cook until the broth is reduced by half. Strain the broth with a fine mesh colander. Add the crushed coffee beans and juniper berries to broth. Return to the heat until you are left with a dark and tasty sauce that you will strain once more. Leave aside to cool.

Fill ¾ of a large saucepan with water, adding 0.5 fl oz (15 g) vinegar, 0.8 fl oz (25 ml) wine and a little salt. Place over a medium heat. When it comes to a boil, add the escargots with their shell and cook for 60 minutes. Drain the escargots and extract them from their shell. Eliminate the black part of the intestines and wash the escargots under cold running water. Return the escargots to the heat and bring them to a boil as you did before, with the same ingredients, for another 60 minutes. Boil the shells in water and bicarbonate for 10 minutes. Mix and soften the butter adding the chopped tarragon, breadcrumbs, a crushed garlic clove (without the germ), salt and some freshly ground black pepper. Place the escargots in the shells and seal them with a layer of the herby butter. Place the escargots in the fridge for a few minutes until the butter becomes firm. Return the sauce to the heat and bring it to a boil. Gradually pour in the potato starch while stirring well with a whisk to prevent any lumps. Preheat the oven to 370 °F (190 °C) and bake the escargots for 10 minutes then place them on a platter with the sauce and some watercress sprouts on the side.

MARINATED MACKEREL WITH KATSUOBUSHI AND PORCINI MUSHROOM SOUP

SERVES 4

4 MACKEREL FILLETS
1 OZ (30 G) KATSUOBUSHI
3.5 OZ (100 G) MISO PASTE
1 ORGANIC LEMON
1 ORGANIC ORANGE
1 OZ (30 G) COFFEE BEANS
6.7 FL OZ (200 ML) EXTRA VIRGIN OLIVE OIL
2 OZ (60 G) SOY SAUCE
0.7 OZ (20 G) DRY PORCINI MUSHROOMS
0.7 OZ (20 G) WHITE WINE
1 BAY LEAF
1 BUNCH OF PARSLEY
SALT TO TASTE

PREPARATION TIME: 45 MINUTES

Grate the lemon and orange zest and mix into the miso paste. Use the mixture to cover each mackerel fillet on the meat side. Squeeze half the lemon and the orange. Pour the juices in one container and mix together. Place the mackerel fillets in the juice skin-side down and leave them to marinade for 12 hours in the fridge.

Rinse the mackerels under some running water to remove the miso paste. Pat them dry with some absorbent paper and sprinkle some salt on the meat side. Heat the olive oil in a pan. Place the mackerel fillets skin side up and then place the pan in the oven preheated to 175 °F (80 °C) for 20 minutes.

Soak the dry porcini mushrooms in warm water for 20 minutes, then drain them removing any earthy residues. Put the mushrooms in a saucepan with 16 fl oz (500 ml) of water, the wine, soy sauce, bay leaf, crushed coffee beans, and 0.7 oz (20 g) of Katsuobushi. Boil for 5 minutes and then sift.

Pour the hot broth in the bowls and add the mackerels skin-side up. Garnish with a few drops of oil, some parsley leaves, and a few Katsuobushi flakes.

COFFEE LASAGNE WITH PECORINO CHEESE, RICOTTA AND OCTOPUS COOKED IN CURRY SOUP

SERVES 4

14 OZ (400 G) RICOTTA CHEESE
5.2 OZ (150 G) GRATED PECORINO CHEESE
3.5 OZ (100 G) GRATED PARMESAN CHEESE
2.2 LB (1 KG) OCTOPUS
0.3 OZ (10 G) CURRY
1 LEMON
1 CLOVE OF GARLIC
16.9 FL OZ (500 ML) WHIPPING CREAM
1.7 OZ (50 G) BUTTER
14 OZ (400 G) STRONG ALL-PURPOSE FLOUR (FLOUR TYPE 0)
3 LARGE EGGS
0.7 OZ (20 G) FINELY GROUND COFFEE
SALT AND PEPPER TO TASTE
EXTRA VIRGIN OLIVE OIL TO TASTE

PREPARATION TIME: 45 MINUTES

Put the flour, coffee and eggs into a planetary mixer and mix. Wrap the mixture with cling film and put in the fridge for 30 minutes.

Clean the octopus, leave it in water for 15 minutes, remove the eyes, beak and innards. Place in a pan, cover with water, add the curry, lemon cut in half, and the unpeeled garlic clove. Bring to the boil, lower to a gentle heat for 40 minutes. Drain and leave to cool in ice and water. Cut off the ends of the tentacles put aside for the garnish, cut the rest of the tentacles into thin rounds, brown them in a non-stick pan with a little oil. Cut the octopus into rounds too.

Slice the lasagne mixture and with a rolling pin roll the slices to a 0,05 in (1 mm) thickness, grease the mono-portion molds with butter and brush the sides with a little cream. Cut the pasta to fit the mold and line the mold. Mix the ricotta with salt and pepper, then alternate the lasagne sheets covered in a layer of ricotta, pecorino cheese, a little octopus, Parmesan cheese and butter with a few teaspoons of cream. The tentacle rounds are placed on the last layers. The last layer is covered with butter, cream and cheeses.

Bake in preheated oven to 370 °F (190 °C) for 18 minutes, grill the top cheese layer.

Serve the lasagne hot and garnished with octopus tentacle tips.

PACCHERI STUFFED WITH CLAM MOUSSE INFUSED IN COFFEE WITH PEA CREAM AND SPROUTS

SERVES 4

11.2 OZ (320 G) PACCHERI
4.4 LB (2 KG) CLAMS
3.5 OZ (100 G) SHELLED PEAS
A SMALL BUNCH OF PEA SPROUTS
10 COFFEE BEANS
3.5 OZ (100 G) POTATOES
2 EGG WHITES
5.2 OZ (150 G) WHITE WINE
A FEW PARSLEY LEAVES
SALT
EXTRA VIRGIN OLIVE OIL TO TASTE

PREPARATION TIME: 1 HOUR

Peel the potatoes and cook in salted water for 40 minutes on a gentle heat.

Wash the clams in plenty of cold water, move them around to completely eliminate the sand, then leave them in a little salty water for 15 minutes. Pour the oil into a pan and brown the parsley, coffee beans and drained clams. Pour in the wine, simmer and reduce, cover the pan. Cook for 3 minutes from boiling. Leave to cool at room temperature a few minutes then remove the clams from their shells. Filter the cooking liquid and add to the clams.

Add the potatoes and blend to obtain a soft velouté-like sauce. Add the egg whites and blend again. Filter with a strainer and put the mixture in a mousse siphon and add 2 charges, then shake.

Boil the peas in salted water for 2 minutes. Drain and blend with a little cooking water, salt and oil to obtain a smooth cream, filtered through a strainer.

Cook the paccheri in plenty of salted water taking care not to break them. Cook for 1-2 minutes less than the recommended time on the packet. Drain, put them into a bowl and drizzle with oil.

Spoon the pea cream into the plate, fill each facchero with the clam mousse and place onto the cream to form a small tower, cover with pea sprouts.

SUCKLING PIG RAVIOLINI, SEASONED WITH CORIANDER, LEMON, COFFEE POWDER AND MUSTARD SPROUTS

SERVES 4

17 OZ (500 G) FLOUR
19 EGG YOLKS
14 OZ (400 G) SUCKLING PIG SHOULDER
1 SHALLOT
1 CARROT
1 CELERY STALK
1 BAY LEAF
6.7 FL OZ (200 ML) WHITE WINE
1 BUNCH CORIANDER

3 RADISHES
3 EGGS
1 TSP TOMATO PASTE
3 LEMONS
3.5 OZ (100 G) BUTTER
1 SMALL BUNCH OF MUSTARD SPROUTS
0.3 OZ (10 G) FINELY GROUND COFFEE
SALT AND PEPPER TO TASTE
EXTRA VIRGIN OLIVE OIL TO TASTE

PREPARATION TIME: 1 HOUR

Wash and chop the vegetables. Preheat the oven to 360 °F (180 °C). Cut the shoulder into small pieces and brown them in a little oil; add the chopped vegetables and cook for a few minutes. Add the bay leaf, tomato paste and deglaze with the wine. Cover and cook in the oven for 1 hour 30 minutes. If needed add half a glass of water to stop the meat from drying.

Let the meat and vegetables cool and then put them all through the mincer, add the eggs, grated radishes, chopped coriander, salt and pepper, then put the mixture in a pastry bag.

Mix the flour and egg yolks in the planetary mixer until perfectly blended. Wrap in cling film, place in fridge and leave for 30 minutes. Roll out the dough to 1 mm thickness. Put walnut size amounts of meat mixture at a regular distance of 0.7 in (2 cm) on the pastry to form two horizontal rows 0.7 in (2 cm) apart. Fold the borders of pastry over the meat and press with the fingers around the meat filling to seal the raviolini. Place the finished raviolini on a tray lined with baking paper sprinkled with flour. Continue until all the ingredients have been used, then put the tray in the fridge.

Melt the butter in a small pan without letting it boil and add the grated lemon zest. Using a whisk slowly add 3.5 oz (100 g) of water until a well-blended cream forms. Season with salt and pepper and place in the fridge.

Cook the raviolini in salted boiling water for 2 minutes, drain and place in a non-stick pan and mix with the butter cream, add a few tablespoons of water if necessary to make them shiny.

Serve the raviolini in soup plates, add the mustard sprouts and sprinkle with the coffee.

GORGONZOLA RISOTTO AND BRITTLE WITH FINE SAVORY COFFEE CRUMBLE WITH CHARD AND TOMATO POWDER

SERVES 4

1 BUNCH GREEN CHARD (ABOUT 10/12 LEAVES)
3 TOMATOES
12.3 OZ (350 G) CARNAROLI RICE
7 OZ (200 G) SWEET GORGONZOLA
4.2 OZ (120 G) GRATED PARMESAN CHEESE
2.7 FL OZ (80 ML) WHITE WINE
1.7 OZ (50 G) BUTTER
SALT TO TASTE
EXTRA VIRGIN OLIVE OIL TO TASTE

FOR THE BRITTLE:
2 EGG WHITES • 1.7 OZ (50 G) BUTTER • 1.7 OZ (50 G) STRONG ALL-PURPOSE FLOUR (FLOUR TYPE 0) • 0.3 OZ (10 G) INSTANT COFFEE • A PINCH OF SALT

FOR THE FINE COFFEE CRUMBLE:
2.1 OZ (60 G) ALMOND FLOUR • 2.1 OZ (60 G) STRONG ALL-PURPOSE FLOUR (FLOUR TYPE 0) • 4 OZ (115 G) BUTTER • 0.7 OZ (20 G) INSTANT COFFEE • 0.1 OZ (5 G) SUGAR 0.1 OZ (5 G) HONEY

PREPARATION TIME: 45 MINUTES

Wash the tomatoes and score a cross on the bottom of each tomato. Blanch them in plenty of boiling water for 10 seconds, then immediately plunge them into icy water to cool. Peel them, cut them into quarters and remove the seeds. Put the tomatoes in the microwave for 5 minutes at 400 W to dry.

Wash and dry the chards, cut off the stalks. Place each leaf on a plate and put in the microwave for 2 minutes at 400 W. Repeat if the leaf is not tender. Dry all the leaves then crush them and press them through a sieve together with the tomatoes.

For the brittle put room-temperature soft butter in a bowl, add the flour, egg whites, coffee and salt, whisk well until the ingredients take on an even coffee color. Pre-heat oven to 360 °F (180 °C). Cover baking tray with baking paper and place small 0,08 in (2 mm) high 3.9x1.5 in (10x4 cm) strips of cream on the tray. Bake in oven for 8 minutes.

For the fine coffee crumble put the room-temperature softened butter in a bowl with the coffee, sugar, honey and mix and blend well. Add a spoonful at a time of the mixed flours stirring well to obtain a grainy crumbly mixture. Spread onto a baking tray lined with baking paper and bake in the oven at 320 °F (160 °C) for 20 minutes. Every 5 minutes work the mixture to keep it flat, especially at the center so that it bakes evenly. Remove from the oven, let it cool at room temperature, the crumble should now be crunchy.

Pour 2 gal (8 l) of lightly salted water into a large saucepan and bring to the boil. Put 3 tablespoons of oil in another saucepan and brown the rice with a pinch of salt. Stir the rice continually to brown it evenly, deglaze with the wine until completely evaporated. Add a few ladles of boiling water and continue stirring. Cook the rice for 14 minutes adding hot water little by little, do not add too much water, the risotto must be rather dry when cooked. Add the butter, stir, add the gorgonzola and Parmesan cheeses, stir until the risotto becomes creamy.

Spoon the hot rice into the plates, add the tomato and chard powders, the fine coffee crumble and serve. Serve the coffee brittle on the side so it maintains its crispiness.

PUMPKIN AND STAR ANISE VELOUTE SAUCE WITH COFFEE AND RASPBERRY LAYER

SERVES 4

8.8 OZ (250 G) RASPBERRIES
2.0 OZ (80 G) SUGAR
JUICE OF HALF A LEMON
17.6 OZ (500 G) SKINNED AND SEEDED PUMPKIN
1 STAR ANISE
0.7 OZ (20 G) BUTTER
0.1 OZ (5 G) FINELY GROUND COFFEE
SALT TO TASTE
EXTRA VIRGIN OLIVE OIL TO TASTE
GARNISH WITH MARJORAM LEAVES

PREPARATION TIME: 30 MINUTES

Whisk the raspberries with the lemon juice, strain the mixture to eliminate the seeds. Add the sugar and boil until reduced to jam. Spread the mixture on a silpat baking sheet. Heat oven to 170 °F (75 °C) and bake for 3 hours.

Pour 13.5 fl oz (400 ml) of water into a saucepan, add the star anise and boil for 5 minutes. Cut the pumpkin into small pieces and cook in the butter for 5 minutes.

Strain the water and star anise, add it to the pumpkin, add a little salt and cook covered on a slow heat for 30 minutes. Cool and then blend to get a shiny smooth velvet sauce.

Serve the hot velvet sauce in transparent bowls, sprinkle some coffee powder and cover with the raspberry layer cut into a circle. Garnish with fresh marjoram leaves and a drizzle of oil.

BROWNED DUCK WITH RED CABBAGE, COFFEE AVOCADO WITH A SCENT OF CUMIN

SERVES 4

2 WHOLE DUCK BREASTS
1 RED CABBAGE
AGAR-AGAR
RED WINE VINEGAR
3 RIPE AVOCADOS
0.1 OZ (3 G) INSTANT COFFEE
½ LEMON JUICE

1.7 OZ (50 G) EXTRA VIRGIN OLIVE OIL
0.1 OZ (5 G) CUMIN SEEDS
0.3OZ (10 G) SOY LECITHIN
3.5 OZ (100 G) CLARIFIED BUTTER
4 SAGE LEAVES
1 ROSEMARY TWIG
SALT AND PEPPER TO TASTE

PREPARATION TIME: 45 MINUTES

Wash and cut the cabbage into pieces, removing the central core. Put in the blender and add 0.1 oz (2 g) of agar-agar every 3.5 oz (100 g) of juice. Mix well with a whisk and bring to a boil. Cool for 3 hours in the fridge. Blend the juice until creamy. Pass it through a sieve, add a little salt, 2 tablespoons of oil and 0.1 oz (3 g) of vinegar every 3.3 fl oz (100 ml) of cream.

Cut the avocados in half and remove the skin. Place the pulp in a bowl and mash until you have a chunky cream. Add the remaining oil, salt, lemon juice and coffee and mix well.

Boil 17 fl oz (500 ml) of water with the cumin seeds for 10 minutes on a low heat. Filter and let it cool. Add the soy lecithin and blend creating a very thick foam.

Separate the duck breasts and make square-like incisions into the skin with a knife. Sprinkle salt and pepper on both sides. Heat a non-stick pan and brown the breasts on the side of the skin without adding any oil. Brown on the other side for 2 minutes over medium heat, adding butter, sage and rosemary.

Put in the oven heated to 370 °F (190 °C) for 5 minutes.

Cut the meat into regular slices and absorb the blood with kitchen paper.

Serve the meat on a thin layer of cabbage cream with some avocado cream and a spoonful of cumin foam on the side. Add a little ground coffee to decorate the dish.

BOAR MORSEL COOKED IN WINE WITH CHOCOLATE AND COFFEE EGGPLANTS

SERVES 4

28 OZ (800 G) BOAR LEG	1 ROSEMARY TWIG
1 CELERY STALK	3 BLACK PEPPERCORNS
1 CARROT	3 JUNIPER BERRIES
1 ONION	1 TSP OF CONCENTRATED TOMATO PUREE
2 GARLIC CLOVES	1 OZ (30 G) BALSAMIC VINEGAR
3.5 OZ (100 G) BUTTER	4 EGGPLANTS
1.7 OZ (50 G) WHITE GRAPPA	4.2 OZ (120 G) 72% DARK CHOCOLATE
1.7 OZ (50 G) CHERRY LIQUOR	0.1 OZ (3 G) INSTANT COFFEE
33 FL OZ (1 L) RED WINE	SALT AND PEPPER TO TASTE
1 BAY LEAF	EXTRA VIRGIN OLIVE OIL TO TASTE

PREPARATION TIME: 45 MINUTES

Dice the boar leg into 2 in (5 cm) cubes, add salt and pepper and brown them on each side with the butter and 3 tablespoons of oil. Finely dice the celery, carrot and onion. Put the vegetables to brown in a large pot with a little oil. Add salt, pepper, rosemary, bay leaf, peppercorns and juniper berries. Let them brown until caramelized. Add the well-browned boar.

Add a little wine to the meat juices and let it evaporate. With a wooden spoon gently scrape the bottom of the saucepan so that the caramelization gives flavor to the wine. Pour the remaining wine and meat juice and wine onto the meat, add 2 glasses of water and the tomato paste. Put the lid on and cook over a very low heat for 2 hours, with the garlic, taking care to keep the meat always moist. Wash the eggplants and cut them in 4 lengthwise. Cook them in the oven at 360 °F (180 °C) for 45 minutes.

Add the vinegar, cherry liquor and grappa to the meat and continue cooking for another 40 minutes until tender. Place the meat on a serving dish and filter the cooking juices with a fine mesh strainer; also squash the vegetables with a spoon to extract all the flavor and then return everything to the heat to thicken the sauce.

Before serving, heat the eggplant pulp again. Add a pinch of salt and 2 tablespoons of oil.

Melt the chocolate in a bain-marie, add the coffee and mix well.

Arrange the meat on one side of each plate, the eggplant on the other, and pour some chocolate and coffee sauce on top.

BEEF SIRLOIN WITH COFFEE POWDER, CHICORY, CAPERS AND CHILI PEPPER

SERVES 4

28 OZ (800 G) BEEF SIRLOIN
0.1 OZ (3 G) FINELY GROUND COFFEE
28.2 OZ (800 G) CHICORY OR PUNTARELLE
15 CAPER BERRIES
2 CHILI PEPPERS
1 GARLIC CLOVE
SALT AND PEPPER TO TASTE
EXTRA VIRGIN OLIVE OIL TO TASTE

PREPARATION TIME: 30 MINUTES

Wash the puntarelle and cut off the shoots of the sprouts, separating them from the smaller and tender leaves. Eliminate the larger leaves.

Blanch the leaves and the chicory in plenty of salted water for 3 minutes, drain and cool in cold water and ice.

Cut 4 slices of sirloin about 1-1.4 in (3-4 cm) thick and add salt and pepper. Pour 3 tablespoons of oil into a non-stick pan. When hot add the meat and brown it. Then transfer the meat to the oven – pre-heated to 390 °F (200 °C) – and roast it for other 4 minutes.

In another saucepan pour a little oil with the unpeeled garlic clove, minced capers and red pepper; brown for 2 minutes on a low heat.

Incorporate the blanched puntarelle without making them brown. Add some salt and sprinkle with coffee.

Cut the meat into small pieces placing them next to the puntarelle. Serve while still hot.

LAMB CUTLETS WITH COFFEE, BLACK PEPPER AND GINGER BREADCRUMB COATING WITH WATERCRESS SALAD

SERVES 4

28.8 OZ (800 G) FRENCHED LAMB SIRLOIN
14 OZ (400 G) PANKO (JAPANESE BREADCRUMBS)
0.7 OZ (20 G) FINELY GROUND COFFEE
4 CRUSHED BLACK PEPPERCORNS
0.1 OZ (20 G) FRESH GINGER
4 EGGS
1.7 OZ (50 G) MILK
5.2 OZ (150 G) STRONG ALL-PURPOSE FLOUR (FLOUR TYPE 0)
10 FL OZ (300 ML) CORN OIL FOR FRYING
1.7 OZ (50 G) CLARIFIED BUTTER
2 BUNCHES OF WATERCRESS
2 LIMES
SALT FLAKES TO TASTE
EXTRA VIRGIN OLIVE OIL TO TASTE

PREPARATION TIME: 45 MINUTES

Cut the meat in 0.7 in (2 cm) thick slices. Lightly grease with oil and place them between two sheets of wax paper. With a meat mallet reduce their thickness to 0.2 in (0.5 cm) and sprinkle some salt on both sides.
Mix the panko with the crushed peppercorns, grated ginger and coffee powder.
Beat the eggs with the milk in a rather large bowl.
Coat the slices of meat with some flour, dip them in the eggs and then coat them with the panko mixture.
Put the butter and the corn oil in a frying pan and fry two slices at a time until golden. Dry them with kitchen paper.
Wash the watercress removing the larger leaves, put aside the whole sprouts that you'll use later for the salad.
Dry the leaves with kitchen paper and dress with the juice of one lime, and the grated zest of the two limes.
Add extra virgin olive oil and salt.
Serve the cutlets on one single platter with the bones on the same side and the salad next to them.

COFFEE MARINATED TUNA WITH EMBER-COOKED CARROTS AND SHISO LEAVES IN COFFEE AND SESAME TEMPURA

SERVES 4

25.3 OZ (720 G) ATLANTIC BLUEFIN TUNA
0.7 OZ (20 G) COFFEE BEANS
1.7 OZ (50 G) SOY SAUCE
0.3 OZ (10 G) RICE VINEGAR
1.7 OZ (50 G) BROWN SUGAR
8 CARROTS WITH THEIR TOPS
16 SHISO LEAVES
0.2 OZ (6 G) FINELY GROUND COFFEE
0.3 OZ (10 G) WHITE SESAME
1.7 OZ (50 G) RICE FLOUR
1.7 OZ (50 G) STRONG ALL-PURPOSE FLOUR (FLOUR TYPE 0)
A PINCH (2 G) OF INSTANT COFFEE
1 BOTTLE OF 17 FL OZ (500 ML) SPARKLING WATER
10 OZ (300 G) PEANUT OIL

PREPARATION TIME: 30 MINUTES

Place 17 fl oz (500 ml) of water in a saucepan and add the coffee beans, vinegar, soy sauce, and sugar and boil for 3 minutes. Filter and leave to cool.

Cut the tuna in about 1 in (3 cm) thick slices and leave them in the cold vinegar and coffee marinade for 3 hours.

Mix the flours, sesame seeds and instant coffee. Add the sparkling water (it must be cold from the fridge) pouring it in slowly while stirring. Whisk until you obtain a creamy tempura, not too thick and not to runny. Place it in the fridge to keep cool.

Wash and peel the carrots without removing the green tops. Wrap every carrot in aluminum foil and cook them in the embers of a barbeque grill for 5 minutes on each side.

Remove the tuna from the marinade and pat it dry with kitchen paper.

Heat the peanut oil to 360 °F (180 °C).

Mix the tempura with a whisk, and dip the shiso leaves in it. Fry them one at a time for about 1 minute each until crispy. Pat them with kitchen paper. Sear the tuna in a very hot nonstick pan for a few seconds on each side, leaving it raw, but not cold, on the inside.

Remove the tinfoil from the carrots. On every plate serve one carrot, some shiso leaves and on the side, without any of the ingredients touching, the diagonally cut tuna and then serve.

CHOCOLATE DEMI-SPHÈRE WITH COFFEE MOUSSE AND FINE COFFEE CRUMBLE

SERVES 4

FOR THE CHOCOLATE DEMI-SPHÈRE:
10 OZ (300 G) 72% DARK CHOCOLATE

FOR THE COFFEE MOUSSE:
14 OZ (400 G) WHIPPING CREAM
0.5 OZ (15 G) COFFEE POWDER
2.8 OZ (80 G) SUGAR

FOR THE COFFEE FINE CRUMBLE:
7 OZ (200 G) SOFT FLOUR (00 TYPE FLOUR)
3 OZ (90 G) BUTTER
3 OZ (90 G) SUGAR
0.5 OZ (15 G) COCOA POWDER
0.8 OZ (25 G) COFFEE POWDER

PREPARATION TIME: 30 MINUTES

Melt the chocolate in a bain-marie at a temperature of 120 °F (50 °C). Remove it from the heat making it reach 82 °F (28 °C) and then bring it back to 88 °F (31 °C). This procedure will make the chocolate bright and shiny. Inflate 4 mini balloons and dip them half way into the melted chocolate. Place the balloons on a small baking tray and store in the refrigerator for 30 minutes. When the chocolate is cold, deflate the balloons and you should have the chocolate demi-sphères you will then use as bowls for the cream and mousse.

For the coffee mousse, in a kitchen boule mix the cream, coffee, sugar and pour the mixture into a mousse siphon. Shake well and add 1 charge. Leave it to set in the fridge for 2 hours.

For the fine coffee crumble pour the flour into a pot; while stirring add the butter at room temperature, sugar, cocoa and coffee until you have a granular mixture. Place in the oven at 320 °F (160 °C) for 25 minutes, stirring occasionally. Remove from the oven, spread the mixture on a baking sheet and let it cool at room temperature. Spread the fine coffee crumble in a plate, then add the demi-sphère filled with mousse. Sprinkle with some more fine coffee crumble and serve.

CREAM PANNA COTTA
WITH COFFEE SAUCE
AND GRANITA

SERVES 4

FOR THE PANNA COTTA:
14 OZ (400 G) WHIPPING CREAM
7 OZ (200 G) FULL FAT MILK
3.5 OZ (100 G) SUGAR
0.3 OZ (9 G) LEAF GELATIN

FOR THE COFFEE GRANITA:
7 OZ (200 G) ESPRESSO COFFEE
2.8 OZ (80 G) SUGAR
0.3 OZ (10 G) HONEY

FOR THE COFFEE SAUCE:
8.8 OZ (250 G) ESPRESSO COFFEE
3.5 OZ (100 G) CASTER SUGAR
0.7 OZ (20 G) BUTTER
0.3 OZ (10 G) CORNSTARCH

PREPARATION TIME: 1 HOUR

For the panna cotta, soak the leaf gelatin in cold water for a few minutes, drain it, squeeze it and pour it into a saucepan with milk, cream and sugar. Bring the mixture to a boil and strain with a colander. Distribute it in transparent glass molds and store in the refrigerator for 3 hours.

For the granita pour 7 oz (200 g) of water in a saucepan, add the coffee, sugar and honey, stir and cook over a gentle fire bringing it to a boil. Pour the mixture into an oven pan and leave it in the freezer for 1 hour.

Stir the mixture, break it up with a fork and then put it back in the freezer. Repeat the operation until it has the consistency of a granita.

For the coffee cream, mix the butter and cornstarch in a saucepan until you obtain a soft mixture; while mixing add the sugar and coffee. Place over the heat and bring to a boil for 1 minute, then place in the refrigerator for 2 hours covering it with cling film.

Mix it thoroughly with a whisk, then pour it on each mold to form a coffee disc of about 5 mm on the surface. Put the granita in a separate cocotte and serve.

PEARS IN VANILLA AND COFFEE SYRUP
WITH YOGURT WAFERS
AND LICORICE POWDER

SERVES 4

FOR THE PEARS:
12 PEARS
1 VANILLA POD
0.2 OZ (8 G) CRUSHED COFFEE BEANS
17 FL OZ (500 ML) WHITE WINE
1 LICORICE ROOT
LEMON ZEST TO TAST

FOR THE YOGURT WAFERS:
9.1 OZ (260 G) SOFT FLOUR (00 TYPE FLOUR)
9.1 OZ (260 G) FULL FAT YOGURT
2 EGGS
1 EGG YOLK
4.2 OZ (120 G) SUGAR
1 PACKET OF ACTIVE DRY YEAST

PREPARATION TIME: 30 MINUTES

Peel the pears and cut the base so that they stand perfectly; place them in a deep pan and add the vanilla, coffee beans, white wine, 17 fl oz (500 ml) of water and lemon zest. Cook for 50 minutes over a gentle flame, allowing the syrup to simmer. Remove the pears and reduce the remaining syrup by one third. Filter it and then pour it back onto the pears.

Grate a licorice root with a fine grater and put the powder aside in a saucer.

Whisk the eggs, egg yolk, and sugar and then add the yogurt. In a bowl mix the flour and baking powder. Sift them and gradually add them to the wet ingredients. Preheat the oven to 340 °F (170 °C). Put the mixture in the sac à poche and squeeze it on a baking sheet covered with parchment paper shaping 3x1.5 in (8x4 cm) wafers. Bake for about 10-12 minutes.

Before serving, heat the pears. Put them in a serving bowl, pour the reduced sauce over them. Positon the freshly baked wafers on the side and sprinkle a little licorice powder on top.

COFFEE SEMIFREDDO
WITH SORREL, CINNAMON SPONGE
AND CRUMBLE

SERVES 4

FOR THE SEMIFREDDO:
2 EGG WHITES
2.2 OZ (65 G) CASTER SUGAR
0.7 OZ (20 G) WILDFLOWER HONEY
1.7 OZ (50 G) INSTANT COFFEE
8.8 OZ (250 G) WHIPPING CREAM
A FEW SORREL SPROUTS TO DECORATE

FOR THE CINNAMON SPONGE:
1 EGG
2 EGG YOLKS

1.7 OZ (50 G) SUGAR
0.3 OZ (10 G) WILDFLOWER HONEY
1 OZ (30 G) FLOUR
0.7 OZ (20 G) CORN OIL
0.2 OZ (8 G) FULL FAT MILK
0.1 (3 G) CINNAMON POWDER

FOR THE CRUMBLE:
2.4 OZ (70 G) FLOUR
1.2 OZ (35 G) BROWN SUGAR
1.9 OZ (55 G) COLD BUTTER

PREPARATION TIME: 1 HOUR

For the semifreddo, pour the sugar, 1.4 oz (40 g) of water, and honey in a saucepan and stir. Cook over medium heat, reaching a temperature of 250 °F (121 °C). Pour the egg whites into the mixer, slowly add the syrup while still hot and beat until stiff. Continue beating until the egg white has reached room temperature.

Place in the fridge to cool. Whip the cream with the coffee. Stir in the egg whites and place the mixture in the appropriate molds. Freeze at -0.4 °F (-18 °C) for at least 4 hours.

Wash and dry the sorrel sprouts. Place them in a container with a lid, between two sheets of dampened kitchen paper and place in the fridge.

For the cinnamon sponge, mix the egg, egg yolks, sugar and honey in a bowl. Keep stirring and add the oil, milk and cinnamon. Gradually incorporate the sifted flour, avoiding the formation of lumps. Pour the mixture into a mousse siphon with two chargers and leave to cool in the fridge for 4 hours occasionally shaking the siphon. Grease the ice-cream cups with a little corn oil. Squirt the cinnamon foam into the cups filling them slightly more than half and bake in the microwave oven for 1 minute at 800 W. Let the sponge cool and then remove it from the ice-cream cups.

For the crumble, mix sugar, butter and flour until you obtain a very grainy lumpy dough. Pour into a pan and bake at 320 °F (160 °C) for 20 minutes turning it occasionally to cook evenly.

Arrange the semifreddo in the center of the plate, surrounding it at the base with some foam. Add the sorrel, its fresh acidic notes will beautifully complement the cinnamon. Sprinkle with some crumble to add the right crunchiness to the dessert.

COFFEE SOUFFLÉ
WITH COFFEE
AND JUNIPER GELATO

SERVES 4

FOR THE COFFEE AND JUNIPER GELATO:
5 EGG YOLKS
3.5 OZ (100 G) CASTER SUGAR
17.6 OZ (500 G) MILK
LEMON ZEST TO TASTE
8 CRUSHED JUNIPER BERRIES
0.5 OZ (15 G) INSTANT COFFEE
1 VANILLA POD
17.6 OZ (500 G) WHIPPING CREAM

FOR THE SOUFFLÉ:
7.7 OZ (220 G) MILK
1.7 OZ (50 G) FLOUR
0.2 OZ (8 G) INSTANT COFFEE
1.5 OZ (45 G) BUTTER
3 EGG YOLKS
3 EGG WHITES
2.1 OZ (60 G) CASTER SUGAR

PREPARATION TIME: 45 MINUTES

For the gelato, whisk the egg yolks and sugar in a bowl. Heat the milk with the lemon zest, coffee, 4 crushed juniper berries and the vanilla bringing it almost to a boil. Pour the milk into the egg yolk mixture, stirring well to avoid lumps.

Put the bowl in a bain-marie and bring the mixture to 180 °F (82 °C), always stirring with a rubber spatula, so that it does not stick. Stir in the whipping cream, stir and leave to cool in the fridge for 4 hours until very cold; filter with a strainer.

Put the mixture directly in the ice cream maker to solidify, or else leave it in the freezer until solid. Cut the mixture into cubes and whisk it to make it creamy gelato.

For the soufflé, melt the butter in a saucepan and, while stirring gradually add the flour. Let it fry for 1 minute and then stir in the cold milk all at once. Keep whisking to avoid lumps. Bring to a boil and simmer for 3 minutes, stirring well, then add the coffee.

After a few minutes add the egg yolks and sugar; beat the egg whites until stiff and incorporate them. Grease and flour the molds, fill them just over half and bake them in a preheated oven at 390 °F (200 °C) for 20 minutes. Pulverize the leftover juniper berries.

Remove from the oven and immediately serve the soufflés without taking them out of their molds while they are still puffed up. Place the gelato in a cocotte and sprinkle it with some juniper powder.

ALPHABETICAL INDEX
OF RECIPE INGREDIENTS

THE AUTHORS

LUIGI ODELLO, Enologist, journalist, founder of Odello Associati, President of Italian Tasters and of the International Institution of Coffee Tasters, CEO of Narratori del Gusto, Istituto Eccellenze Italiane Certificate and Istituto Internazionale Chocolier and General Secretary to the Italian Espresso National Institute, Academic Secretary to the International Academy of Sensory Analysis, member of the Board of Directors of Absis Consulting and Grappa National Institute, and director of *L'Assaggio*, *Sensory News*, *Coffee Taster* and *Grappa News*.

During his career, Luigi Odello has gained specific experience in sensory analysis and in the implementation of corporate innovation with particular focus on neurolinguistic organization and transactional analysis. He has carried out 300 hours a year of university lectures, he is thesis advisor or co-advisor of over 90 theses and author of numerous publications.

He has written 19 books, collaborated with the most important sector magazines and delivered reports in numerous conventions in Italy and abroad.

FABIO PETRONI As a professionally trained photographer, Fabio Petroni has collaborated with the most established professionals in the sector, specializing in portraits and still life. Over the years, he photographed leading figures in the world of Italian culture, medicine, and economy. He works with the main advertising agencies and is the author of several campaigns for prestigious and internationally renowned firms and companies. He personally curates the image of important Italian brands. He is the official photographer for the IJRC - International Jumping Riders Club and for the Young Riders Academy.

He has signed several prestigious publications with White Star Publishers.
www.fabiopetronistudio.com

GIOVANNI RUGGIERI, was born in Bethlehem in 1984 but grew up in Piedmont. He has trained professionally in many "starred" kitchens, such as those of the Piazza Duomo in Alba and the Scrigno del Duomo in Trento. Now chef of the Refettorio Simplicitas, a restaurant of polished elegance in the heart of the Brera district of Milan, Ruggieri is devoted to spreading a newly rediscovered approach to food based on simplicity, with a strong emphasis on the quality of raw materials: these are selected on the basis of seasonality and authenticity. Ruggieri's dishes and flavors follow the most authentic traditions, using anew many of the niche products to be found in his region. His is a simple style of cuisine, sober, balanced and, in its way, almost ascetic.

HOW TO LEARN COFFEE TASTING

The International Institute of Coffee Tasters (Iiac) is a nonprofit association only supported by its member subscriptions. Its aim is to study and spread scientific methods for sensory evaluation of coffee. It has always focused on espresso, the symbol of made in Italy, perfecting a specific tasting method. Since its creation in 1993, Iiac has carried out hundreds of Italian Espresso Tasting courses, attended by operators and coffee lovers from all over the world. In 1999, Iiac created the Italian Espresso Specialist course to certify operators working in coffee shops serving Certified Italian Espresso. In 2005, the Professional Master's Degree in Coffee Science and Sensory Analysis was inaugurated. In 2012, the Italian Espresso Trainer program was created to train ambassadors of Italian coffee. Iiac's research activities are supported by a high level scientific committee. The Italian Espresso Tasting manual is available in Italian, English, German, French, Spanish, Portuguese, Russian, Japanese, Chinese, Thai and Korean.
Information on courses and activities can be found at: *www.assaggiatoricaffe.org*.

BIBLIOGRAPHY

Luigi Odello, Carlo Odello, *Espresso Italiano Tasting* (edition I), Centro Studi Assaggiatori, 2001
Luigi Odello, Carlo Odello, *Espresso Italiano Tasting* (edition II), Centro Studi Assaggiatori, 2017
Luigi Odello, *Espresso Italiano Roasting,* Centro Studi Assaggiatori, 2009
Luigi Odello, *I cru del caffè,* Centro Studi Assaggiatori, 2013
Luigi Odello, Manuela Violoni, *Sensory analysis. The psychophysiology of perception*, Centro Studi Assaggiatori, 2017
Silvano Bontempo, *Dal chicco alla tazzina un piacere senza confini,* L'Assaggio
Manuela Violoni, *Il cappuccino italiano certificato,* L'Assaggio
Francesco and Riccardo Illy, *The Book of Coffee: A Gourmet's Guide*, Abbeville Pr, 1992
Antonio Carbè, *Il caffè nella storia e nell'arte* (seconda edizione), Centro Luigi Lavazza
Maria Linardi, Enrico Maltoni, Manuel Terzi, *Il libro completo del caffè*, DeAgostini, 2005

PHOTO CREDITS

All photographs are by Fabio Petroni except the following:

page 8 Jeremy Woodhouse/Blend Images/Getty Images
page 13 Nattika/Shutterstock
page 16 Robert George Young/Getty Images
pags 18-19 Maximilian Stock Ltd./Getty Images
page 20 Ann Ronan Pictures/Print Collector/Getty Images
pages 22-23 Nenov/Getty Images
page 24 Fine Art Images/Heritage Images/Getty Images
page 25 Neil Fletcher & Matthew Ward/Dorling Kindersley/Getty Images
page 27 Jesse Kraft/123RF
page 28 Reza/AGF/Hemis
pages 40-41 John Coletti/Getty Images
pages 42-43 Dick Davis/Science Source/Getty Images
pages 44-45 Ed Gifford/Royalty-free/Getty Images
page 46 Alvis Upitis/Passage/Getty Images
page 48-49 Ze Martinusso/Moment Open/Getty Images
page 50-51 Oleksandr Rupeta/NurPhoto/Getty Images

page 52-53 Paula Bronstein/Getty Images
pages 54-55 Bartosz Hadyniak/E+/Getty Images
page 57 Bill Gentile/Corbis Documentary/Getty Images
pages 58-59 Reza/Getty Images
pages 60-61 Reza/Getty Images
pages 64-65 Reza/Getty Images
page 74 alextype/123RF
page 76 Robert Przybysz/123RF
pages 78-79 Vladimir Shulevsky/StockFood Creative/Getty Images
page 156 Evannovostro/Shutterstock
page 163 republica/E+/Getty Images
page 165 Popperfoto/Getty Images
page 189 ansonsaw/E+/Getty Images
page 191 StockFood/Getty Images

Cover and backcover bottom: Joseph Clark/Getty Images

ACKNOWLEDGEMENTS

The Editor wishes to thank for their valuable collaboration in the making of this book:
MILANI S.p.A. and Elisabetta Milani for their dedication in carrying out the photo shoot.
Mumac Academy and Gruppo Cimbali S.P.A., and Luigi Morello and Filippo Mazzoni for their support in realizing the pictures.
The Taster Study Centre.
Simone Bergamaschi, assistant to Fabio Petroni.
Davide Canonica, kitchen assistant.
Villa Giù of Faggeto Lario, Como for Chef Giovanni Ruggieri's recipes.

WHITE STAR PUBLISHERS

WS White Star Publishers® is a registered trademark
property of White Star s.r.l.

© 2018 White Star s.r.l.
Piazzale Luigi Cadorna, 6 - 20123 Milan, Italy
www.whitestar.it

Translation and editing: Langue&Parole, Milan (traduction: Karen Tomatis)

ISBN 978-88-544-1305-4
1 2 3 4 5 6   22 21 20 19 18

Printed in Italy by Rotolito S.p.A. - Seggiano di Pioltello (Milan)